CAMBRIDGE LIBRARY COLLECTION

Books of enduring scholarly value

Naval and Military History

This series includes accounts of sea and land campaigns by eye-witnesses and contemporaries, as well as landmark studies of their social, political and economic impacts. The series focuses mainly on the period from the Renaissance to the end of the Victorian era. It includes major concentrations of material on the American and French revolutions, the British campaigns in South Asia, and nineteenth-century conflicts in Europe, such as the Peninsular and Crimean Wars. Although many of the accounts are semi-official narratives by senior officers and their relatives, the series also includes alternative viewpoints from dissenting leaders, servicemen in the lower ranks, and military wives and civilians caught up in the theatre of war.

An Account of the Campaign in the West Indies, in the Year 1794

The naval chaplain Cooper Willyams (1762–1816), who was educated at Emmanuel College, Cambridge, and took holy orders in 1784, published this account of the West Indies campaign in 1796. The son of a navy commander, Willyams was also a self-taught artist and topographer, and in 1802 published his eyewitness account of the battle of the Nile, also reissued in this series. The campaign against the French in the Caribbean was notable for the large numbers of combatants on both sides who succumbed to yellow fever. Using his own notes and the accounts of other eyewitnesses, Willyams describes the arrival of the fleet, commanded by Sir Charles Grey and Sir John Jervis (later Earl St Vincent, for whom Willyams acted as chaplain), in Barbados; the actions undertaken against the French to secure the islands of Martinique, St Lucia, and Guadeloupe; and the subsequent recapture of the latter by the French.

Cambridge University Press has long been a pioneer in the reissuing of out-of-print titles from its own backlist, producing digital reprints of books that are still sought after by scholars and students but could not be reprinted economically using traditional technology. The Cambridge Library Collection extends this activity to a wider range of books which are still of importance to researchers and professionals, either for the source material they contain, or as landmarks in the history of their academic discipline.

Drawing from the world-renowned collections in the Cambridge University Library and other partner libraries, and guided by the advice of experts in each subject area, Cambridge University Press is using state-of-the-art scanning machines in its own Printing House to capture the content of each book selected for inclusion. The files are processed to give a consistently clear, crisp image, and the books finished to the high quality standard for which the Press is recognised around the world. The latest print-on-demand technology ensures that the books will remain available indefinitely, and that orders for single or multiple copies can quickly be supplied.

The Cambridge Library Collection brings back to life books of enduring scholarly value (including out-of-copyright works originally issued by other publishers) across a wide range of disciplines in the humanities and social sciences and in science and technology.

An Account of the Campaign in the West Indies, in the Year 1794

*With the Reduction of the Islands of Martinique,
St. Lucia, Guadaloupe, Marigalante, Desiada, &c.*

Cooper Willyams

CAMBRIDGE
UNIVERSITY PRESS

CAMBRIDGE
UNIVERSITY PRESS

University Printing House, Cambridge, CB2 8BS, United Kingdom

Cambridge University Press is part of the University of Cambridge.
It furthers the University's mission by disseminating knowledge in the pursuit of
education, learning and research at the highest international levels of excellence.

www.cambridge.org
Information on this title: www.cambridge.org/9781108083812

This edition first published 1796
This digitally printed version 2015

ISBN 978-1-108-08381-2 Paperback

AN
ACCOUNT

OF THE

CAMPAIGN IN THE WEST INDIES,

IN THE YEAR 1794,

UNDER THE COMMAND OF THEIR EXCELLENCIES

LIEUTENANT GENERAL SIR CHARLES GREY, K.B.

AND

VICE ADMIRAL SIR JOHN JERVIS, K.B.

COMMANDERS IN CHIEF IN THE WEST INDIES;

WITH

THE REDUCTION

OF THE

ISLANDS OF MARTINIQUE, ST. LUCIA, GUADALOUPE, MARIGALANTE, DESIADA, &c.

AND THE EVENTS THAT FOLLOWED THOSE UNPARALLELED SUCCESSES,
AND CAUSED THE LOSS OF GUADALOUPE.

By the Rev. COOPER WILLYAMS, *A.M.*

VICAR OF EXNING, SUFFOLK,

AND LATE CHAPLAIN OF HIS MAJESTY'S SHIP BOYNE.

LONDON:

PRINTED BY T. BENSLEY;

FOR G. NICOL, BOOKSELLER TO HIS MAJESTY, PALL-MALL; B. AND J. WHITE,
FLEET-STREET; AND J. ROBSON, NEW BOND-STREET.

1796.

TO

GENERAL SIR CHARLES GREY,

KNIGHT OF THE MOST HONOURABLE ORDER OF THE BATH,

AND

ADMIRAL SIR JOHN JERVIS,

KNIGHT OF THE MOST HONOURABLE ORDER OF THE BATH, AND COMMANDER
IN CHIEF OF HIS MAJESTY'S FLEETS IN THE MEDITERRANEAN,

THIS SHORT ACCOUNT

OF

THEIR BRILLIANT EXERTIONS IN THEIR COUNTRY'S CAUSE,

IS MOST RESPECTFULLY DEDICATED BY

THEIR OBEDIENT

AND GRATEFUL HUMBLE SERVANT,

EXNING, AUGUST 10, 1796.

COOPER WILLYAMS.

PREFACE.

———

WHEN an author lays his book before the public, unless it be a work of genius, some account of his motives for so doing is generally expected. As this is a work that pretends to nothing but authenticity, and to be a plain relation of facts, I shall only premise, that, placed in a situation which gave me an opportunity of being witness to most of the principal transactions of the expedition under Sir CHARLES GREY and Sir JOHN JERVIS in the West Indies, and having leisure and inclination to minute down the occurrences as they presented themselves, I venture to appear before the public with such humble pretensions alone, as the result of that opportunity and leisure can give me.

My original intention reached no further than to publifh a few views of fome interefting fubjects, which abound in the Caraibean Iflands; but I felected thofe only which were rendered moft fo by particular events. Though I pretend not to the powers of an artift (being felf-taught), yet I beg leave to urge in excufe for that want of fpirit and picturefque effect which, I fear, is but to apparent in my drawings, that they are fcrupuloufly exact, and accurately delineate the fubjects they profefs to reprefent.

When I at firft communicated my defign of publifhing a few drawings, taken during the Weft India Expedition, many of my friends, and fome of the officers who ferved with me, knowing that I had kept a journal of the tranfactions, defired me to add a fhort account of them to accompany the engravings.

To thofe, at all converfant with writing fuch accounts, it will not appear ftrange, that, as I proceeded to retrace thofe events which form the moft prominent feature of my life, I found a pleafure in recognifing many a tranfaction that had almoft faded from my memory, and by degrees it increafed under my hand, till it became of fize fufficient to form a volume, and I was enabled to lay it before the public in a more refpectable form than I at firft intended. But, that I may not appropriate to myfelf merit belonging to another, I take a pleafure in avowing, that through the kindnefs of an officer, who, from his rank, is not more confpicuous than refpected by the general tenor of his conduct, I have been favoured with the affiftance of a journal by an ingenious and active officer of his divifion, which has greatly contributed to the embellifhment of my work, by the communication of many local circumftances, impoffible for me otherwife to have been acquainted with. The like affiftance I have alfo to acknowledge from a friend who ferved under General Prefcott during his gallant defence of Fort Matilda.

By the favour and indulgence of the Commander in Chief, I have been permitted to make extracts from the public order-book of the army; thefe form a large appendix, which, I truft, will not only confirm the accuracy of my narration, but will prove both ufeful and entertaining to the army in general.

Such has been the origin and progrefs of this publication; to the candour, therefore, of the public I commit myfelf, trufting that, as my ambition has been humble, I fhall not be expofed to the feverity of literary criticifm for not having obtained that which I have never attempted.

CONTENTS.

CHAPTER I.

CHAPTER II.

CHAPTER III.

CHAPTER IV.

CONTENTS.

CONTENTS.

CONTENTS.

CHAPTER XI.

CHAPTER XII.

CHAPTER XIII.

LIST

OF

SUBSCRIBERS.

His Royal Highnefs Field Marſhal the Duke of York.

A

Charles Abbott, Efq. Queen's Square, Bloomſbury.

John William Adams, Efq.

..... Armit, Efq. Army Agent, Dublin.

Colonel Harvey Aſton, 12th regiment.

Lieutenant Colonel Aſtley, Norfolk light dragoons, Burgh Hall, Norfolk.

J. P. Allix, Efq. Swaffham Court, Cambridgeſhire.

Richard Allnutt, Efq. South Park, Penſhurſt, Kent; two copies.

Mr. Alken, No. 2, Francis Street, Gower Street.

B

Right Honourable Lord Blaney, Lieutenant Colonel 66th regim.

Honourable Captain Charles Boyle, 62d regiment, Aid-de-camp to the Lord Lieutenant of Ireland.

Colonel Brownrigg, Coldſtream regiment of guards.

Lieutenant Colonel Bayley.

Thomas Barrett, Efq. Lee, near Canterbury.

I. Bargrave, Efq. Eaſtry Court, Kent.

LIST OF SUBSCRIBERS.

S. Baker, Efq. Lynn Regis, Norfolk.

James Rickard Barker, jun. Efq. Swaffham, Cambridgeſhire.

Reverend Dr. Bates, Freckingham.

Major Barnard, New Romney light dragoons.

Henry Bell, Efq. Wallington, near Downham, Norfolk.

Colonel Blackwood, 33d regiment light dragoons.

William Boys, Efq. F. R. S. and F. S. A. Sandwich, Kent.

Mr. Boys, Eaſtry, Kent.

Rev. Edward Tymewell Brydges, Wootton Court, Kent.

Lieutenant Colonel Brydges, New Romney light dragoons.

Samuel Egerton Brydges, Efq. F.S.A. Denton Court, Kent, Captain in the New Romney light dragoons; two copies.

Mrs. Brydges, Precincts, Canterbury.

Mrs. Bryant, Exning, Suffolk.

Mrs. Breton, Gogmagog Hills, near Cambridge.

Lieutenant Colonel Brereton, 63d regiment.

Lieutenant Samuel Brown, New Romney light dragoons.

Major Burnet, 43d regiment.

Mr. Brome, Dublin Caſtle.

. . . . . Blades, Efq.

Mr. Benſley, Bolt Court, Fleet Street.

C

His Grace John Lord Archbiſhop of Canterbury; two copies.

His Excellency Earl Camden, Lord Lieutenant of Ireland.

The Right Hon. Lieutenant Colonel, Viſcount Conyngham.

Colonel Lord Clements.

Colonel Sir Edward Crofton.

Honourable Lieutenant Colonel George Lowry Cole.

Right Hon. General Cuningham, Commander in Chief in Ireland.

Right Honourable William Burton Conyngham.

Brigadier General Cradock, Quarter Maſter General in Ireland.

Lieutenant General Croſbie.

Reverend Edward Cage, Eaſtlinge, Kent, Chaplain to the New Romney light dragoons.

Reverend Thomas Cookes, Barbourne Houſe, Worceſterſhire.

Mrs. Cookes.

Lieutenant Henry Cookes, New Romney light dragoons.

LIST OF SUBSCRIBERS.

Mr. Thomas Secundus Cookes, of his Majesty's ship St. George.
Mr. Denham Cookes, Worcester college, Oxford.
Mr. Charles Cookes.
Colonel Coote, 70th regiment.
Mrs. Coote.
. . . . . Coote, Esq.
Christopher Cooke, Esq. Beaufort Buildings, Strand.
T. Collingwood, Esq. Gray's Inn.
Rev. T. Cogan, East Deane, Surry.
Thomas William Coke, Esq. Holkham, Norfolk.
Lieutenant Colonel Crosbie, 22d regiment, and Deputy Adjutant General in Ireland.
Robert Cromp, Esq. Frinsted, Kent.
Mr. John Cruikshank, Rector of the Academy in Banff.

D

Right Honourable Lord Delaval.
Reverend Dr. Dering, Prebendary of Canterbury.
Col. Cholmely Dering, New Romney light dragoons.
John Thurlow Dering, Esq. Crow Hall, Norfolk; two copies.
Captain Donkin, 44th regiment.

E

Right Honourable Mr. Elliott, Secretary at War, Ireland.
Edward Everard, sen. Esq. Lynn Regis, Norfolk.

F

Right Honourable Earl Fitzwilliam; two copies.
Honourable Edward Foley, M. P. Lower Seymour Street.
Mr. Farringdon, Foulkes Buildings, London.
Miss Farringdon, Camberwell.
Mrs. Faulknor.
Lieutenant Colonel Fisher, 9th regiment, Manchester Square.
Captain Finlay, Richmond House.
Lieutenant Foster, 38th regiment.
Reverend Dr. Frampton, D. D. Exning, Suffolk.

G

General Sir Charles Grey, K.B. three copies.
Right Honourable Lord Glentworth.
Sir Henry Grey, Baronet, Howick, Northumberland.
Lady Gresley, Drakelow, Derbyshire.

LIST OF SUBSCRIBERS.

Sir Robert Goodere, Cavendish Square.
Mrs. Goodere, Exning, Suffolk.
W. Gordon, Efq. Aberdour, Banff.
Charles Grey, Efq. M. P. Hertford Street, Mayfair; two copies.
Mrs. Grey, Hertford Street, Mayfair.
Lieutenant Colonel Henry Grey, 18th regiment light dragoons.
Major Thomas Grey, 39th regiment.
Captain George Grey, Commander of his Majefty's fhip Victory.
Captain William Grey, 21ft regiment.
Edward Gregory, Efq. Leman Street, Goodman's Fields.
J. Græme, Efq.
George Gipps, Efq. Canterbury.
Ifaac Gervais, Efq. Doctors Commons.

H

Sir Henry Harpur, Baronet, Upper Brook-ftreet.
Sir Benjamin Hammett, Knight, Lombard Street.
Major General Hewitt, Adjutant General of Ireland.
Mrs. Harrifon, Bourne Place, Kent.

Major Hare, 12th regiment light dragoons, Aid-de-camp to the Lord Lieutenant of Ireland.
Mr. K. S. Haggerftone, Cambridge.
Chrift. Hand, Efq. Cheveley Green.
Reverend James Hand, Cheveley, Cambridgefhire.
C. J. Harford, Efq. Stapleton, Gloucefterfhire.
Henry Wife Harvey, Efq. Hearnden, Kent.
Captain John Harvey, of his Majefty's fhip Prince of Wales.
Mr. George Gerard Haughs.
Mrs. Herring, Precincts, Canterbury.
Reverend J. Hippifley, A.M. Stow on the Wolde, Gloucefterfhire.
Reverend Thomas Hey, D. D. of Wickham Breux, Kent.

J

Admiral Sir John Jervis, K. B. Commander in Chief in the Mediterranean; three copies.
Chriftopher Jefferfon, Efq. Dullingham, Cambridgefhire.
Henry Jackfon, Efq. 106, Fenchurch Street, London.
Major General Johnfon.

LIST OF SUBSCRIBERS.

K

Honourable George King, Colonel of the Cork regiment of militia.

George Kittoe, Efq. Ridge Houfe, Antigua.

Sir Edward Knatchbull, Bart. M. P. Marfham Hatch, Kent.

L

His Grace the Duke of Leinfter.

Right Honourable Lady Charlotte Lenox.

Honourable Colonel Lenox.

Sir William Lemon, Baronet, M. P. Carelew, Cornwall.

John Lagier Lamotte, Efq.

Mr. Henry Lamotte, Clapton, Middlefex.

Captain Locke, 26th regiment light dragoons.

Reverend Dr. Lynch, Archdeacon and Prebendary of Canterbury.

Rev. William Long, LL.D. Sternfield, Suffolk.

Reverend Daniel Lyfons, F.R.S. and F. S. A. Putney, Surrey.

Mr. W. H. Lunn, Bookfeller, Cambridge; four copies.

Rev. N. C. Lane, A. M. Chrift's College, Cambridge.

M

Lady Mill, Arlingham, Gloucefterfhire.

Brigadier General Myers.

Lieutenant Colonel Manley, royal artillery.

Lieutenant Col. M'Clary, Aberlafh, Carmarthenfhire; two copies.

Lieut. Col. Madden, 15th regiment.

Lieutenant Colonel M'Donald.

Sir Charles Mitchell, Knt. Commander of the William Pitt Eaft Indiaman.

Mr. James Miln, Arbroath.

N

Major General Needham.

Reverend James Nafmith, A.M. Leverington, Cambridgefhire.

Reverend Edward Nares, A.M. Fellow of Merton College, Oxford.

Mr. Norton, Bookfeller, Briftol.

O

William Owen, Efq. Trinity College, Cambridge.

P

Right Hon. Sir John Parnell, Chancellor of the Exchequer, Ireland.

LIST OF SUBSCRIBERS.

James Palmer, Efq. Dulwich, Surry; two copies.

Reverend Dr. Pennington, D. D. Eaftry, Kent.

Rev. Montagu Pennington. A. M.

Mr. Philpot, Canterbury.

George Ponfonby, Efq. Bifhop's Court, near Dublin.

J. Plumptre, Efq. Fridville, Herts.

Reverend Charles Powlett, A. M. junior, Hackwood Farm, Hants.

Edward Roger Pratt, Efq. Ryfton Hall, Norfolk.

Lieutenant Colonel Pratt, royal Irifh artillery.

Captain D'Arcy Prefton, royal navy.

George Purvis, Efq. Titchfield, Hants, Secretary to Admiral Sir John Jervis.

Major Perryn, Great George Street.

R

Reverend Anth. Luther Richardfon, LL. B. Kennet, Cambridgefhire.

Mr. James Robertfon, Gellymell, near Banff.

William Rofe, Efq. Mountcoffer, near Banff.

E. Rolfe, jun. Efq. Hankoe, Norfolk.

S

Right Hon. Lord Sondes, Rockingham Caftle.

Colonel Sir James St. Clair Erfkine, Bart. 12th reg. light dragoons.

Charles Henry Selwyn, Efq. Lieutenant Governor of the ifland of Montferrat.

Reverend George Selwyn, King's Road, Bedford Row.

Matthew Henry Scott, Efq. Captain in the royal navy.

W. Sharpe, Efq. Fulham, Middlefex.

Samuel Shirt, Efq. 27, Mincing Lane, London.

Rev. Stebbing Shaw, B. D. F. S. A. Fellow of Queen's College, Cambridge.

Reverend Mr. Alexander Simpfon, Old Aberdeen.

Rev. Thomas Jenyns Smith, A. M. Firft Fellow of Dulwich College.

Mr. David Souter, Melrofe, near Banff; five copies.

Mr. Stewart Souter, Duff Houfe, Banff.

Lieutenant Colonel Stuart, 3d regiment guards.

Rev. James Symes, Hollis Street.

Powell Snell, Efq. Guiting Grange, Gloucefterſhire, and Captain of the royal Gloucefterſhire yeomen cavalry.

Richard Sill, Efq A.B. Clare Hall, Cambridge.

T

Right Honourable the Earl of Tyrconnel.

George Talbot, Efq. Temple Guiting, Gloucefterſhire.

T. Tyndall, Efq. Wefton Lodge, Somerfetſhire.

Captain Thomas, 28th regiment.

Captain Herbert Taylor, 2d dragoon guards, and Aid de Camp to his Royal Highneſs the Duke of York.

Captain Edward Taylor, New Romney light dragoons.

Mr. William Thompſon, Mile-End Green.

Mrs. Treacher, Henley on Thames.

Reverend Stephen Tucker, A. M. Linfted, Kent.

John Townley, Efq. Clare Hall, Cambridge.

Lieutenant Colonel Thewles, 30th regiment light dragoons.

V

Captain George Vaughan, of the royal navy.

Mrs. Vernon, Norwich.

Captain Vaumorel, 30th regiment.

W

Colonel, the Earl of Weftmeath.

Sir Charles Watſon, Baronet, Swaffham, Cambridgeſhire.

Sir Edward Winnington, Bart. M.P. Winterdyne, Worcefterſhire.

Major General Whyte.

Mrs. Watſon, Swaffham, Cambridgeſhire.

Mr. J. Webfter, Merchant, Banff.

Charles Hollis Weftern, Efq. M. P. Felix Hall, Effex.

Edw. Weatherby, Efq. Newmarket.

Thomas M. Waller, Efq. Lieutenant royal navy.

Samuel Whitbread, fen. Efq. M. P.

Samuel Whitbread, jun. Efq. M. P. 17, Lower Grofvenor Street; two copies.

Rev. Edward Wilſon, B. D. Moulton, Suffolk.

Mrs. Willyams, Exning, Suffolk.

John Hanbury Williams, Efq. Coldbrook, Monmouthſhire.

LIST OF SUBSCRIBERS.

Major Wilder, Pall Mall.

Captain Isaac Wolley, royal navy.

Reverend Godfrey Wolley, Hutton Bushel, Yorkshire.

J. Whatley, Esq. Wraxall Lodge, Somersetshire, and Captain in the Royal South Gloucestershire regiment of militia.

James Wyborn, Esq. Hull, Kent.

. . . . . . Western, Esq.

Mr. Thomas Henry Wilson, No. 13, Cornhill.

EXPEDITION

AGAINST THE

FRENCH WEST INDIA ISLANDS.

CHAPTER I.

EXPEDITION TO THE WEST INDIES DETERMINED ON....SIR CHARLES GREY AND SIR JOHN JERVIS APPOINTED COMMANDERS IN CHIEF....THE BOYNE SAILS FROM SPITHEAD....OCCURRENCES ON THE VOYAGE FROM THENCE TO CARLISLE BAY, BARBADOES.

In the latter end of the year 1793, his Majesty having determined to send a formidable armament to the West Indies, to reduce the French islands in that quarter, and to secure his own from any attack of the enemy, Lieutenant General Sir Charles Grey, Knight of the Bath, was promoted to the rank of General in America, and Commander in Chief in the West Indies. Several officers of distinguished abilities were also appointed to act under him; and Vice

B

Admiral Sir John Jervis, Knight of the Bath, was nominated Commander in Chief of the naval force on the fame expedition.

After much delay, occafioned by nearly half the original force being withdrawn from the armament intended for the Weft Indies, and applied to another purpofe, on the 24th of November, 1793, the Boyne of 98 guns, Captain Grey commander, having Vice Admiral Sir John Jervis's flag flying at the fore-topmaft head, made the fignal for failing to the fleet deftined with her for this expedition, and dropped down to St. Helen's, where fhe lay at fingle anchor, waiting for thofe fhips that were not ready; the ordnance ftorefhips were particularly tardy. This morning an unfortunate accident befel Mr. Scott, fecond lieutenant of the Boyne, whofe arm was broken by a block giving way in the fore part of the fhip, where he was ftationed; but happily, by the care and fkill of Mr. Weir the furgeon, he was nearly recovered by the time the fhip reached Barbadoes.

On Tuefday the 26th of November the Boyne weighed anchor, and with the reft of the fleet failed from St. Helen's with a fair wind down channel. On the 27th we lay to off Portland Road, waiting for the Quebec frigate, which remained at Spithead to haften the ftorefhips and tranfports (that were not at firft ready to fail with the Boyne), and to convoy them through the Needles.

On the 28th of November, in the morning, we were off the Land's End, and were foon afterwards becalmed for a fhort time. In the evening, a frefh breeze fpringing up, we proceeded on our voyage. Before it was dark eight fail were feen from the maft head.

On the 29th we paffed Commodore Paifley in the Bellerophon, with feveral frigates in company. The Commodore faluted the Admiral's flag with thirteen guns, which was returned from the Boyne with eleven guns.

As it may be proper to inform the reader that, in confequence of a particular invitation from the Admiral, the Commander in Chief and his fuite, with feveral of the officers on the ftaff under him, were paffengers in the Boyne, I fhall here fubjoin their names.

His Excellency Sir Charles Grey, K. B. Commander in Chief.

Major General Thomas Dundas.

Lieutenant Colonel Symes, Quarter Mafter General.

Major Henry Grey, Deputy Quarter Mafter General.

Lieut. Col. Fifher, Secretary to the Commander in Chief.

Major Lyon, Deputy Adjutant General.

Captain Finch Mafon,
Lieut. John Cunningham, } Aid de Camps to the Commander in Chief.
Captain Newton Ogle,

Capt. Maitland, Aid de Camp to Major General Dundas.

Dr. Wardle, Surgeon on the Staff.

Alfo Chevalier Sancée, a brave and ingenious French Officer, whom the Commander in Chief took with him, as being acquainted with the ifland of Martinique, and the fortifications of Fort Bourbon and St. Louis, having ferved under the Marquis de Bouillé at the conftruction of the former works.

Thus, by the friendly intercourse fubfifting between the two Commanders in Chief, the time on the paffage was moft ufefully employed in forming plans of operation, which could not have been executed with that promptnefs that diftinguifhed the enfuing campaign, had it been otherwife.

On Tuefday the 3d of December, the Rofe frigate, Captain Riou, parted company; as did, on the 7th following, Commodore Thompfon and part of the convoy, and we proceeded with the greater difpatch on our voyage.

On the 8th of December the wind proved foul, with rain and hazy weather. At night, in the middle watch, we were attacked by a fquall of wind and rain, accompanied by a heavy fea, which ftruck the rudder with fuch violence, that the men at the wheel lofing their hold, were thrown down; and the tiller breaking loofe, ftove in the gunner's cabin; at the fame time the pinnace, a fix-oared boat, that was fufpended over the ftern, was wafhed away, and totally loft.

On the 9th of December in the morning, the fhip was taken aback by a fudden fquall of wind, attended with thunder and lightning, with a moft tremendous fea; we then wore fhip, and ftood to the fouth weft. Thofe who have never failed in a fhip of war of the firft or fecond rate, can form no idea of the grandeur and awfulnefs of the fcene when fo large a body is ftruggling with contending elements. As the fhip rolls through the high fwell her fides appear to twift and bend in a furprifing manner. The guns hanging on one fide, and preffing againft the other, feem as if, at every roll, they would, by their immenfe weight, force their way through; which, added to the cracking of the cordage, the roaring of the wind, and a variety of other noifes, forms a fcene of furprife and alarm to the inexperienced voyager.

This fqually weather continued at intervals for four days. On the 12th we faw fome fea gulls. On the 13th two ftrange fail hove in fight; the Ulyffes chafed one of them, and we made fail after the other, and fired feveral fhot at her to bring her to; but in the evening were obliged to give up the purfuit, for fear of parting from our convoy, which however happened in the following night, during a heavy gale of wind.

On Saturday the 14th we faw a gull, and feveral turtle paffed near the fhip.

On the 16th land was difcovered at four P. M. fuppofed to be the ifland of Porto Santo. All this day we failed at the rate of feven and eight knots an hour. Tuefday the 17th of December we found that during the night we had paffed by the ifland of Madeira; but this morning tacked and ftood towards it, and arrived off Funchial, the capital of that ifland, of which we had a delightful view. As we approached the land the furrounding country had a very beautiful appearance, efpecially after a long voyage, when the eye has been wearied by the uninterefting famenefs of an extended ocean. The town of Funchial, fo named from the Portuguefe word funcho, fennel, which grows in great abundance on the neighbouring rocks, is fituated at the bottom of a bay, and is a large ill-built town: it has many churches and convents; but as we did not go on fhore, I can give no particular defcription of them. Immediately behind the town the hills rife gradually one above the other, terminating in prodigious high mountains, which are plentifully covered almoft half-way up with plantations of vines, interfperfed with churches and elegant houfes. High up in the mountains, in a valley is feen a convent, which we were informed is dedicated to our Lady of the Mountain. All the buildings being white, formed very confpicuous, and not un-pleafing objects in the landfcape. The mountains in this ifland are very high. Pico Ruevo is fuppofed to be from its bafe near a mile in perpendicular height, much higher than any land in England or Wales. The fides of all the hills are well covered to a certain height with vines, above which, to a vaft extent, are woods of pine, chefnut, and a variety of other trees unknown to Europe. The principal refrefhments to be procured here are wine, water, and onions; the latter are the fineft in the world, and in great plenty.

It being the Admiral's determination to lofe no time, we only lay-to off Funchial, till the wine intended for the ufe of the officers and fhip's company was taken on board; and it being the birth day of the Queen of Portugal, we faluted the fort in honour of the day with twenty-one guns, which was returned with an equal number. In the evening we made fail for our deftination; and fortunately from this time had a fair wind till we got into the trades. On the 24th we paffed the tropic of Cancer, lat. at noon 23. 21. N. long. 32. W. The ufual ceremony was obferved by

the crew (having firſt obtained the Captain s permiſſion): a gro-
teſque Neptune and Amphitrité were drawn by their attendants
on the quarter-deck, where, after a ſolemn ditty chaunted by his
aquatic majeſty, the uſual collections were made, which, from the
munificence of the General and his friends, together with the
contributions of thoſe officers of the ſhip who had never croſſed
the tropic before, amounted to a ſum ſufficient to ſupply the
ſhip's company with plenty of vegetables on their arrival at Barbadoes.

The 25th of December, being Chriſtmas day, divine ſervice
was performed on the quarter-deck by the Chaplain, the crew ap-
pearing as on a Sunday, in clean trowſers and jackets: and here
I muſt beg leave to mention, that I never ſaw more regularity and
decorum in any place of worſhip than is invariably obſerved on
board of his Majeſty's ſhips of war.

This day we paſſed an American brig; and the weather being
fair, Lieutenant Bowen and Captain Maſon went on board her.
She was from Cadiz, and reported, that yeſterday ſhe paſſed a
Spaniſh man of war bound for Europe.

On the 26th of December we ſaw ſeveral albicores, dolphins,
and grampus, and ſhoals of flying fiſh; lat. at noon 22. 10. N.
long. 34. 46. W.

On the 29th of December, being Sunday, and the weather
fair, divine ſervice was performed as uſual.

The heat of the climate now began to be troubleſome to thoſe
who had been unaccuſtomed to it.

On Monday the 6th of January, 1794, land was difcovered from the maft-head, which proved to be the ifland of Barbadoes; and by noon the Boyne anchored in Carlifle Bay[a].

[a] On our arrival we found feveral of the fhips that had parted company on the voyage; and each day after brought more of them, till the whole were collected.

CHAPTER II.

THE COMMANDERS IN CHIEF PREPARE FOR THE EXPEDITION
AGAINST MARTINIQUE.... GUN-BOATS CONSTRUCTED, AND
DESCRIBED.... A SHORT ACCOUNT OF BARBADOES .... SALE
OF SLAVES.... A LIST OF THE FLEET.

THE firſt news we received on our arrival at Barbadoes was, that
the yellow fever had, in the courſe of laſt year, carried off fifty-
eight officers of the army in this and the neighbouring iſlands,
and privates in proportion. It proved fatal to great numbers of
the inhabitants alſo of Barbadoes; from fifteen to twenty whites
died daily in the town of Bridgetown, and about half that number of blacks and people of colour. We were at the ſame time
comforted with an aſſurance that the diſeaſe had entirely ſubſided;
but the reader will ſoon ſee how fallacious were our hopes in this
reſpect. Alas! too many families have to lament the fatal effects
of this dreadful diſorder; and the kingdom at large may attribute
to it the loſſes we afterwards ſuſtained, rather than to any other
cauſe. But of this more hereafter.

His Excellency Sir Charles Grey landed at Bridgetown on the
7th of January, and reſided at a houſe called the Government

c

Houfe, on Conftitution Hill, a healthy fituation, about half a mile out of town, where he was bufily employed during his refidence on the ifland in concerting plans for future operations, in reviewing the troops, and providing againft thofe exigencies which in an enemy's country an army muft be expofed to. A report was here circulated that General Rochambeau the commanding officer at Martinique, and Bellegarde the popular leader of the people of colour, were at variance; but this news by no means caufed the leaft relaxation on the part of our commanders, who continued their preparations with as much ardour as before; and it is well they did fo, as we afterwards found the enemy on their guard, and prepared to refift us with their united force.

The Admiral in the mean time was equally employed in preparing every thing in his department, and for that purpofe remained on board (a conduct he invariably followed), by which every thing was carried on under his own infpection, and delay (the confequence of neglect) was thus prevented.—On our voyage, whenever the weather permitted, a certain number of feamen were exercifed, and formed into companies, to be commanded by lieutenants of the navy, with the rank of captains on fhore. While in Carlifle Bay thefe feamen were again exercifed, and inftructed in the ufe of fmall arms and pikes. This plan of training the feamen for fhore duty was highly beneficial on this expedition, as will hereafter appear.

Every exertion was now made both by fea and land. The gun-boats, which were conftructed in England, then taken to pieces, and brought to the Weſt Indies in ſtoreſhips, were put together with as much ſpeed as poſſible; yet, from the nature of their ſtructure, could not be finiſhed until a day or two before we failed. There were ſix gun-boats, each carrying a twenty-four pounder in the bow, which moved backwards and forwards on a groove: round the whole on the gun-whale was a moveable barricade or breaſt-work, compoſed of ſeveral folds of bulls' hides, nailed to ſome boards of an inch thick in partitions, and capable of turning a muſket ball. Each boat had two maſts; the foremaſt inclined forward (to give more room for the gun to recoil), and had a latine ſail and jib: the mizen was a lug-ſail. Sweeps, or large oars, were alſo ſupplied, to be uſed when there was no wind, or when becalmed by the high lands near the ſhore. Each of theſe veſſels was at firſt commanded by a midſhipman, who, as his conduct merited, was promoted to the rank of lieutenant[b].

In the mean time the troops were landed from the tranſports, the ſick comfortably lodged in the hoſpitals, and every attention paid, to render the ſervice complete. As the major part of our army conſiſted of the flank companies, great pains were taken by the commanding officers to train them for the moſt active ſervice: the light infantry were exerciſed daily by Major General Dundas, who had, in America and on the continent, diſtinguiſhed himſelf at the head of that battalion. Particular attention was paid to inſtruct the army in the abſolute neceſſity of ſtrict obe-

[b] I have given an exact repreſentation of one of theſe boats in the view of the town and bay of St. Pierre.

dience to orders; for which purpofe the Commander in Chief publifhed in the general orders to the army fuch full and comprehenfive inftructions, as to preclude the neceffity of multiplying them in future, and to take away the poffibility of any one pleading ignorance of them[c].

Before we quit this ifland, it may be agreeable to the reader to have fome account of it, and of the general appearance of the country. Barbadoes is fituated in 13. 10. N. lat. and 59. W. long. from London. It is called one of the Britifh Charaibé Iflands, though at prefent none of thofe ancient inhabitants remain on it. The ifland has a flat appearance; but, from the variety of plantations, the beauty and frefhnefs of the verdure, and the numerous houfes, mills, and other buildings, fcattered in great profufion, it prefents a delightful profpect to ftrangers on their approach to it after a long voyage. I fhall not pretend to give an hiftory of the ifland, but muft refer the reader to the elegant work of Bryan Edwards, Efq. whofe account of the Britifh Weft India Iflands is written with every advantage to be derived from local refidence and connections, as well as from the indefatigable attention and abilities of the author.

During our refidence at this ifland curiofity led me to be prefent at a fale of flaves, juft imported from the coaft of Africa. As this horrid traffic in human flefh has been the topic of public inveftigation for fome time paft, and much learning and ingenuity has been difplayed on both fides of the queftion, I fhall not give

[c] See in the Appendix, page 1.

any opinion on it, but merely state facts that came within my own knowledge. The fale is proclaimed by beat of drum, and is held (at Barbadoes at leaft) not in the open air, as I had been taught to believe, but in a commodious houfe appointed for that purpofe. At the time I am fpeaking of, there were about forty men, women, and children, fitting on benches round a large room, with no other covering than a cloth round their waifts. Some of them were decorated with beads, given to them by their captors, and bracelets round their wrifts and ancles, and were much tattooed on their faces and breafts, which I underftood from a feaman who came with them, was a mark of diftinction in their own country. I was alfo informed that they had buried one hundred and forty-nine on the paffage, having had a very bad and protracted voyage : the crew had fuffered equally, and had buried one third of their original complement. As foon as the planter has fixed on a flave he retires with him and the falefman to another room, there concludes the bargain, and departs with his purchafe to his plantation, where the new comer, being clothed in a coarfe jacket, and provided with a hat, knife, and other trifles, is placed with one of the old negroes, by whom he is inftructed in his bufinefs. In regard to the feverity exercifed by the flave owners on their flaves, whatever may have been the cafe, I am well affured that now there are feldom inftances of thofe cruelties which have been fo feelingly defcribed, at leaft in the iflands we vifited on this expedition. At Barbadoes they appeared to be in as comfortable a fituation as the lower ranks of fociety generally are; and as the climate is peculiarly favourable to poverty (clothes and firing, the great articles of expence to the poor in other countries, being here hardly required), I may venture to affirm, that the flaves in the Weft Indies are in a better fituation, *as to the neceffaries of life*, than the labouring poor in England, or any other country in Europe. Far be it from me, however, to juftify flavery in itfelf; it moft certainly is an evil: but when a matter of great importance is in agitation, every information fhould be obtained, and both fides of the queftion ought to be ftrictly examined. Certainly the benevolent intentions of the friends to the abolition of flavery in the Weft Indies have, by their exertions in the caufe of humanity, occafioned a more minute inquiry into the fituation of the flaves than had ever been made before; and feveral excellent laws to re-gulate the treatment of that unfortunate clafs of human beings have in confequence been paffed in the different iflands. It is affirmed by many very humane people, that the entire abolition of the traffic *itfelf* would not help the caufe of humanity fo much as was at firft contended (for I believe the former plan of imme-diately emancipating thofe already imported, is allowed by all to be dangerous in the extreme); and it is the opinion of many writers, that the greater part of thofe Africans fold to our plan-tations would remain flaves in their own country, or be put to death by their captors. If fo, furely it is better for them to be carried to a country where they have a chance at leaft of better treatment, and where many of them are inftructed in their duty to their God, of which before they had no idea.

While we were lying in Carlifle Bay the fleet that failed with us from Europe, and parted company on the voyage, came in, together with the tranſports, &c. from Ireland. The following is, I believe, a correct liſt of the men of war that compoſed our fleet at the commencement of the campaign. A few others that are hereafter mentioned joined us in the courſe of it.

Boyne ..... 98 guns { Vice Admiral Sir John Jervis, K. B. Commander in Chief of the naval force in the Weſt Indies. Captain G. Grey.

Vengeance 74 .... { Commodore C. Thompſon. Captain Henry Powlett.

Irrefiſtible 74 .... John Henry.

Veteran ... 64 .... Charles Edmund Nugent.

Blanche ... 32 .... Chriſtopher Parker.

Terpſichore 32 .... Samſon Edwards.

Blonde .... 32 .... John Markham.

Solebay ... 32 .... William Hancock Kelly.

Beaulieu ... 40 .... John Saliſbury.

Quebec ... 32 .... Joſias Rogers.

Roſe ...... 23 .... Edward Riou.

Veſuvius bomb .... Charles Sawyer.

Nautilus ... 18 .... James Carpenter.

Rattleſnake 18 .... Matthew Henry Scott.

Seaflower .. 16 .... William Pierrepoint.

Zebra	18 guns	Captain Robert Faulknor.	
Experiment . . .	44	. . . . . . Simon Miller.	
Woolwich	44	. . . . . . John Parker.	armed
Dromedary	44	. . . . . . Sandford Tatham.	en flute.

These ships joined us in Fort Royal bay during the siege of Forts Bourbon and Louis.

Afia	64 guns	Captain John Brown.
Santa Margarita	36	. . . . . . Eliab Harvey.
Affurance	44	. . . . . . Velters Cornwall Berkley.
Ceres	32ʼ	. . . . . . Richard Incledon.
Winchelfea	32	. . . . . . Lord Vifcount Garlies.
Roebuck	44 hofp. fhip.	. . . . . Andrew Chriftie.

The land force employed on this expedition was as follows. A detachment of white and a detachment of black light dragoons, three battalions of grenadiers, three battalions of light infantry, the fixth, ninth, fifteenth, thirty-ninth, forty-third, fifty-fixth, fifty-eighth, fixty-fourth, fixty-fifth, and feventieth regiments, with detachments from the fecond, twenty-firft, and fixtieth regiments. The troops were divided into three brigades; the firft commanded by Lieutenant General Prefcott, the fecond by Major General Thomas Dundas, and the third by Major General his Royal Highnefs Prince Edward (till whofe arrival from Canada the command of this brigade was given to Lieutenant Colonel Sir

Charles Gordon. The total force that embarked for the attack of Martinique was fix thoufand and eighty-five, two hundred and twenty-four fick, and nine hundred and feventy-feven left fick at Barbadoes [e].

[e] An idea was ftarted of raifing four hundred white men in the ifland of Barbadoes to augment the army; but there was not time to arm and difcipline them; therefore it was dropped. However, a certain number of negroes were provided to attend the army, four hundred of whom were fent from Dominica for that fervice; fome more were brought from St. Vincent's; and the council of Barbadoes made an offer of fupplying a large number of them to ferve on very liberal terms; but when the matter came to be inveftigated, the terms were found to be far from equitable, and therefore were rejected.—Mr. Baillie and Mr. Monro, two planters of Grenada, were here introduced to the Commanders in Chief, and were received on board the Boyne as guefts, and treated with the greateft hofpitality; they proceeded with us on the expedition. Mr. Gibbs, one of the council of Barbadoes, alfo accompanied us.

MAP
of the Island of
MARTINIQUE
for an Account of the Expedition
against the
French West India Islands,
by the Rev.d Cooper Willyams A.M.

Explanation
- Town or Houses
- Sugar Works
- Water Mills
- Battery
- Battery inland
- Anchorage
- Roads

Scale of British Miles
1 2 3 4 5 6 7 8 9 10

Engraved by S.I.Neele 352 Strand London.

Published July 1.st 1806, by the Rev.d Cooper Willyams.

61° Longitude West from London.

G.t la Caravelle
P.te la Caravelle
Pt.e Chateau
Diamond Dundas
landing here Feb.t 5.th 1794
Gillian Bay
Islet Haussieur
Robert Town
R. Alezard
French Town
Pit.ns du Vauclain
Vauclain
Marin Bay
Pilot
French Bay
Iron au Chat
R. Salée
St Luce
Cape S.t Thomas
Grande Anse D'Arlet
P.t Bargeau
Anse D'Arlet
Diamond Point
Diamond Rock
Pigeon Estate
the Fleet
anchored here Feb.t 12 1794
Fort Royal
Cul de Sac
P.t du Marin
S.t Anne
P.t Tartis
Great
Salt Pit
Salines
Islands
Cape Ferre
Fort Edward or Macabau
Trinite Vaudan
Macabau Bay
Bay of the Galleon
Town & Bay of S.t Pierre
Mont Pelé
Morne aux Bœufs
P.t Negro
la Oase Pilot
P.t du Jacob
Gros de Navires
Morne du Jacob
R. Capot
Morne Jacob
Morne de l'Olive
S.t Mary
Town of la Trinité
Trinité Bay
Bourg du Gros Morne
Carbet
Le Dubourg
P.t Ribbon
La Roger
Manacabou
La Grand Riviere
La Perle
Scale of British Miles

CHAPTER III.

THE FLEET SAILS FROM BARBADOES....ANCHORS ON THE SOUTH COAST OF MARTINIQUE....CAPTURE OF A BATTERY ....GENERAL GREY LANDS WITH HIS ARMY....FLAG OF TRUCE FIRED ON BY THE ENEMY....THE COMMANDERS IN CHIEF ATTACK THE ISLAND AT THREE DIFFERENT PLACES AT THE SAME TIME.

On Monday, Feb. 3, 1794, the fleet of men of war, tranſports, ſtoreſhips, &c. ſailed from Carliſle Bay, and the next morning land was ſeen, which proved to be the iſland of St. Lucia, bearing weſt ſeveral leagues. On Wedneſday, Feb. 5, we approached the iſland of Martinique on the ſouth eaſt coaſt, off the bay of Maran; two forts, one at Pointe du Jardin, the other at Pointe de la Borgneſſe, which defended the entrance to that bay, began to fire on our ſhips as they approached; notwithſtanding which, the Boyne and the reſt of the fleet anchored by four P. M. not far from the battery on Pointe de la Borgneſſe, Lieutenant Bowen having previouſly run along ſhore in a ſmall ſchooner to ſound the depth of water. Our troops were now preparing to land, and had filled ſeveral flat-boats which lay along-ſide the men of war, when the battery opened a heavy fire on them, which was quickly anſwered by the ſhips; the troops at the ſame time puſhed in and landed, covered by the gun-boats: ſeeing which, and alarmed by ſome well-directed ſhot from the Boyne and Veteran, the enemy fled in diſorder from the fort, which our troops immediately entered, and having hoiſted the Britiſh colours, were ſaluted with three cheers from the fleet. A trench was found in the battery, communicating with the magazine, in which a train was laid, and a brand or match laid acroſs it. Happily (by the exertions of the officers and men) this daſtardly plot was prevented taking effect. The guns were immediately turned upon the enemy in their retreat, and againſt the town of St. Anne; but as this was a poſt of no great conſequence, after they had ſpiked the guns and broke the carriages, the troops reimbarked[f].

In the evening the enemy in the battery on Pointe du Jardin burnt the ſugar plantations near them, as we ſuppoſe, out of revenge for our ſucceſs at Pointe de la Borgneſſe; from the dryneſs of the canes the fire ſpread with great rapidity, and did much damage. Near us was the village of St. Luce, where a two-gun battery, directed by the curé of St. Luce, ſeeming diſpoſed to trouble us, the Veteran opened her lower deckers on it, and ſoon

---

[f] During the landing of our troops, Lieutenant Bowen, who was in a gun-boat, perceived a number of the enemy collecting in the woods near the ſhore, and being ſcarce noticed by them, was ſuffered to approach without moleſtation, and having loaded his gun with langrege, he dealt ſuch deſtruction among them, that they fled in all directions. A ſhot from the battery, which ſtuck in the larboard bow of the Boyne, when cut out, proved to be a thirty-four pounder, and to have been heated, but not ſufficiently to do any miſchief by fire.

drove the enemy from thence[g].—On Thurſday morning, Feb. 6, our troops landed at Trois Rivieres, in the bay of St. Luce, without oppoſition, to the number of two thouſand four hundred and eighty-four men, under the direction of Lieutenant General Preſcott. Sir Charles Grey and his ſuite then landed, and the whole army moved off from the landing-place in two diviſions; the firſt diviſion began to march about twelve at noon, the ſecond diviſion at five in the afternoon. Lieutenant Rogers of the Boyne ſoon after landed at the curé's battery at St. Luce, and found the two cannon there to be twenty-four pounders, that had belonged to the Raiſonable man of war, wrecked ſome time ſince on this iſland. They deſtroyed theſe guns, and returned on board without any loſs. This evening a gun-boat and flat-boat with ſeamen, under the command of Lieutenants Rutherford and Ogle of the Boyne, and Mr. Johnſon, midſhipman, attempted to cut out ſome veſſels in the harbour near Maran, where they were much expoſed both to the great guns and muſquetry of the enemy; but they ſucceeded ſo far as to bring off two American ſchooners; two others ſaved themſelves by running aſhore cloſe under the guns of Fort St. Etienne.

On Feb. 7th the Admiral ſent (with a flag of truce) Lieutenant Miln of the Boyne, accompanied by Lieutenant James of the fifteenth regiment, and the Chaplain of the Boyne, with a letter

[g] The Generous Friends tranſport, laden with officers' baggage, &c. dragged her anchor on the night of the 5th, ſtruck againſt a rock at the entrance of the bay, and was wrecked. Fortunately, however, the hands on board and the baggage were ſaved.

for the municipality or governor of Maran. As they approached the town they perceived hostile preparations making in the fort of St. Etienne; but, in hopes of preventing a flag of truce being insulted, Mr. Miln boarded one of the American ships that had been run aground the day before, intending, in case the captain of it was on board, to take him in his company. Being now within half gun-shot of the fort, the enemy began to fire on the boat, notwithstanding the flag of truce, and continued to do so, although Mr. Miln endeavoured to proceed towards the shore: but the enemy seeming determined to oppose his landing, and several of their shot falling close by the boat, he at length judged it most prudent to return. As he passed Pointe du Bourgnesse he perceived some negroes near the fort, and sent the two gentlemen who accompanied him armed, to endeavour to cut off their retreat, and to give them the papers which were to have been delivered to the commander at Maran; but the negroes, on perceiving them land, immediately made off towards the town: they however found a wounded man, whose leg had been broken by a cannon ball, with whom they left the papers, adding a note to express their surprise and indignation at a flag of truce being fired on [h].

In the afternoon Mr. Miln went with the gun-boats against Maran, to form a diversion in favour of Lieutenants Rutherford

[h] The French have since said that they fired on the boat because it had a white flag hoisted: this was a most ridiculous objection; for, though with them a mark of aristocracy, it has ever been acknowledged by all nations as a signal of peace and cessation from hostilities. However, we found it necessary afterwards to comply with their wishes; and whenever a boat was sent from either party on a truce, they carried the flag of the opposite party in the bow of the boat, and their own colours abaft.

and Rogers, who had landed with two companies of feamen to carry frefh provifions to Sir Charles Grey's army. This had the defired effect, as foon after a large body of troops came down from the hills to the town and fort, which might otherwife have fallen in with the feamen on their march.

The next day, Feb. 8, the Admiral fent another flag of truce by the fame officer to the town of St. Anne. He took with him an American captain of a fhip, in addition to his former comple- ment; and having been fo roughly handled the day before, he alfo ordered a gun-boat to attend. St. Anne's was entirely de- ferted. The American then proceeded a mile up the country to the houfe of a planter, who had left it; but finding his mulatto miftrefs there, he left the papers with her, to forward to the com- manding officer at Maran. On this eftate the American told us he faw three hundred flaves, and every thing in perfect order; from whence we judged the owner of it had been a friend to the revolution, the houfes and plantations of the royalifts being uni- verfally deftroyed. The enemy now entirely evacuated this part of the country, to throw themfelves into Fort Bourbon; and in their retreat burnt feveral fine plantations, and murdered many flaves of the royalifts with circumftances of the moft horrid cruelty.

I fhould have mentioned that, on our approach to this ifland, the Commanders in Chief difpatched General Dundas with Com- modore Thompfon to the attack of Trinité, and another divifion under the command of Colonel Sir Charles Gordon, affifted by Captain Rogers of the Quebec, to Cafe de Navirre; while Sir

Charles Grey, affifted by Lieutenant General Prefcott, and under cover of the Boyne, &c. made good his landing at Trois Rivieres: thus, by making three attacks upon diftant parts of the ifland at the fame time, the force and attention of the enemy was divided; and by that fpirited conduct, which animated all parties, more particularly by the unanimity which prevailed between the army and navy, they all happily fucceeded. And here I muft beg leave to obferve, that where the commanders are united in friendfhip, and equally infpired with an earneft defire to ferve their king and country, their example will always have fuch influence on the conduct of thofe under their command, that the fame friendly intercourfe will be fure to fubfift between the fubordinate ranks of the two fervices; and, from the Commanders in Chief to the private foldier and failor, they will join hand and heart, and form a phalanx that nothing can withftand.

CHAPTER IV.

MARCH OF THE COMMANDER IN CHIEF FROM TROIS RIVIERES
TO SALLEE.... OCCURRENCES ON THE MARCH.... GENERAL
WHYTE DETACHED.... TAKES PIGEON ISLAND.... THE AD-
MIRAL ANCHORS OFF PIGEON ISLAND.... DESCRIPTION OF
THE BAY OF FORT ROYAL.... THE THIRD BRIGADE LANDS
AT CAS DE NAVIRES.

I HAVE already faid that his Excellency Sir Charles Grey, with
Lieutenant General Prefcott, and that part of the army which
landed at Trois Rivieres, marched from thence on Feb. 6th acrofs
the country to La Riviere Sallée, a diftance of two leagues, over
very mountainous roads, and that evening they reached the town
of the fame name, fituated on its banks, where the troops were
lodged. They met with no oppofition on their march, and loft
only one man (a fergeant), who died of fatigue and heat. On
the march the Commander in Chief detached Brigadier General
Whyte, with the fecond battalion of light infantry commanded
by Lieutenant Colonel Clofe, with two amuzettes, to force the
batteries of Cape Solomon and Point a Burgos, in order to get
poffeffion of Pigeon Ifland, as our fhipping could not go into the

E

bay of Fort Royal till that was accomplished; nor indeed could our boats with provisions and ammunition go with safety round to the army at Riviere Sallée. On Feb. 7th General Whyte took two small pieces of cannon loaded, at a village in the bay of d'Arlet (one hundred and fifty mulattoes having fled at his approach); and immediately marching to the attack of the two posts above mentioned of Point Solomon and Burgos, the enemy surrendered at discretion, their retreat being cut off. In the interim the Commander in Chief received intelligence of a body of the enemy having crossed the bay from Fort Royal, and landed near Morne Charlotte Pied, where they took post to intercept the communication between General Whyte and head quarters at Sallée: on which he instantly dispatched Adjutant-General Colonel Dundas, with the seventieth regiment, commanded by Lieutenant Colonel Johnson, with two howitzers, to dislodge them. This was executed that night with great spirit, and the post taken possession of early the next morning, the enemy being completely defeated at the first charge. In this action Captain Nares of the seventieth regiment distinguished himself so as to gain the notice of the Commander in Chief in public orders[i].

Brigadier General Whyte (being now reinforced with a detachment of the royal artillery, some ordnance, mortars, &c.) Colonel Symes, with a detachment of the fifteenth regiment and two hundred seamen from the Admiral, armed with pikes and pistols, under the command of Lieutenants Rogers and Ruther-

[i] Vide Appendix, page 14.

ford, afcended the heights on the 9th inftant, and got poffeffion of Mount Matharine, which commanded Pigeon Ifland, at the diftance of not more than four hundred yards, where they erected their batteries. On this day his Excellency the Admiral failed from Maran Bay, and anchored in Petite Ance d'Arlet, from whence he could fend fuccours of men and ammunition to General Whyte; who accordingly inftantly landed two companies of feamen, with feveral cannon, which they in vain attempted to drag over the hills to General Whyte's poft, a diftance of four or five miles; for the fteepnefs and ruggednefs of the roads rendered every effort ineffectual. However he fent him a plentiful fupply of fhot and other ammunition, with one howitzer; and in the evening Lieutenant Miln was difpatched with a party, carrying provifions and fpirits for the army. We found the country on the march from Ance d'Arlet to General Whyte's camp beautiful in a high degree, but the roads almoft impaffable: a fucceffion of fteep roads, through thick woods, at length brought us to the fummit of a hill (on which our feamen were pofted), commanding a fine view of the bay of Fort Royal, with Iflet aux Ramieres, or Pigeon Ifland, in front; and on each fide rofe hills finely clothed with wood, on one of which our little army was pofted. During the time we were there, the enemy on Pigeon Ifland annoyed us with their fhells and fhot, by which one of our feamen was killed, and another mortally wounded. The two five and a half inch howitzers, brought by the feventieth regiment from head quarters, being now placed in a battery under the direction of Captain de Rivigne of the royal artillery, fo as to take the ifland in reverfe, and Colonel Dornford having also joined with a company of artificers, the batteries were completed during the night of the 10th inftant, and opened on Tuefday morning, February 11th, under the conduct of Major Manley, who kept up fo inceffant and well directed a fire upon Pigeon Ifland, that in two hours the garrifon ftruck their colours, and furrendered at difcretion, having fifteen killed and twenty-five wounded. When our batteries opened, it confifted of two hundred and three men.

After the ftrong orders the Commander in Chief iffued during the time he was preparing for the commencement of the campaign at Barbadoes, in which, among other things, he declared his determination to punifh with the utmoft feverity any one who fhould prefume to maraud or plunder the inhabitants, it is furprifing that on the firft day's march any foldier fhould have had the temerity to offend againft that order: but we had a melancholy inftance of it in William Milton of the tenth light dragoons, and Samuel Price of the black dragoons, who were tried and convicted of a robbery in the houfe of Jacques, an inhabitant of Sallée; and the General, being determined to put an early ftop to fuch enormities, had the fentence put in execution, and they were both hanged in view of the whole army on February 8th[k].

On the capture of Iflet aux Ramieres, or Pigeon Ifland, the Admiral failed with the reft of his fleet from Ance d'Arlet on

[k] Vide Appendix, pages 10, 11, 12.

Wednefday, Feb. 12th, and anchored in Fort Royal Bay, off
Pigeon Ifland, by which means he could co-operate with his colleague, and fupply the army with ammunition and provifions
at pleafure. As the fhips worked into the bay, feveral fhells were
thrown at them from Fort Louis, but happily without doing any
mifchief.—It is impoffible to conceive a more beautiful fcene than
prefented itfelf on our entrance into this fine bay. On the north
fide we faw Fort Louis and the town of Fort Royal; and immediately behind it, on the top of a fteep hill, was the ftrong
fortification of Fort Bourbon, which, with the tri-coloured flag
waving on its walls, formed a confpicuous object in the landfcape;
the parapet being built of white ftone, ftrongly contrafted with
the vivid glow of verdure on the furrounding hills. To the weft-
ward rofe majeftically prodigious mountains, called Les Pitons
du Carbet, the hills on the fide of which were cultivated, while
the mountains themfelves were covered with wood to their fum-
mits. Eaftward the bay opens to feveral bays and harbours, into
which fome noble rivers difcharge themfelves, and pleafant iflands
of different dimenfions and forms, embellifh the whole. Pigeon
Ifland, or Iflet aux Ramieres, is fituated on the fouth fide of the
bay of Fort Royal, about two hundred yards from the fhore, and
is a fteep rock, inacceffible except on one fide by a ladder fixed
againft a perpendicular wall. The fummit is about thirty yards
above the level of the fea, and is three hundred paces round. It
contained the following ordnance, viz. Eleven forty-two pounders, fix thirty-two pounders, four thirteen-inch mortars, and one

howitzer, with an immenfe quantity of ftores and ammunition, and a large ftove to heat fhot; it alfo had good barracks. It is famous for having prevented Admiral Rodney with twelve fail of the line from entering the bay in 1782.

On the 12th of February the fifteenth regiment, led by Major Lyon, and commanded by Captain Paumier, furprifed feveral hundreds of the enemy, very ftrongly pofted on the heights of le Grande Bouclain, killed feveral of them, and took all their ammunition and arms, with their cattle.[1]

Sir Charles Gordon with the third brigade had landed on the 8th inftant to leeward, on the fide of Cas de Navires, under cover of a divifion of the fleet commanded by Captain Rogers in the Quebec[m]. The enemy being mafters of the grand road and the heights above it, he made a movement towards the mountains, and turning them (unperceived) with part of his force, gained the moft commanding poft in that part of the country. By day-break on the 9th inftant Colonel Myers, defcending the heights, took poffeffion of la Chapelle, and a poft eftablifhed by the enemy above it; and on his return to the column, Sir Charles Gordon proceeded through moft difficult ground to the heights of Berne, above Ance La Haye. The enemy, after having abandoned the battery of Cayman, and fet fire to the village, ftill keeping a con-

[1] Vide Appendix, page 16.

[m] They met with confiderable oppofition in this bufinefs; and the boats employed in landing the troops by fome miftake got clofe under the enemy's batteries, before they difcovered their fituation. Our lofs however was lefs than might have been expected. The Dromedary, venturing too near the battery of Point Negro, received a fhot between wind and water, entering under the counter, and a fecond fhot went through the quarter-deck barricade, killed one man, and wounded four, among whom was Captain Tatham.

ftant fire on him from the batteries of St. Catharine, he took a position which gave him an eafy communication with the tranf-ports; when on the 12th he obferved the battery and works at St. Catharine, and the pofts which guarded the firft ravine, abandoned by the enemy, on which he took poffeffion of them, while Colonel Myers, with five companies of grenadiers and the forty-third regiment, croffed four ravines higher up, feizing all the batteries that defended them. This movement was completely fuccefsful, the enemy flying on every fide, and our troops were foon in poffeffion of the five batteries between Cas de Navires and Fort Royal. They then proceeded, and occupied the pofts of Gentilly, La Cofte, and La Archet, within a league of Fort Bourbon.

CHAPTER V.

WHEN Commodore Thompſon with his diviſion (having on board Major General Dundas and the ſecond brigade) parted from the fleet on their voyage from Barbadoes, he proceeded with the ut-moſt expedition to the north eaſt part of the iſland; and on Feb. 5th arrived off the bay of Gallion. Captain Faulknor in the Zebra led in, and placed himſelf along-ſide of the battery on Point a Chaux, from whence he ſoon drove the enemy. The Beaulieu, Captain Saliſbury, and the Woolwich, Captain Parker, followed; and the troops were landed without further oppoſition about a league from the town of Trinité, which was ſituated on the fur-ther ſide of the iſthmus that formed the bay of Gallion. Here

F

General Dundas halted for that night. Early the next morning he began his march towards Trinité. As he moved off from the ground he had occupied during the night, the enemy annoyed him much by a brisk fire of musketry from the cane fields, where a large body of them were concealed; from thence however they were soon driven by the bayonet, which (as the Commander in Chief observed") in the hands of a gallant British soldier is the first of weapons. In this business we had one artilleryman killed, and two officers and three privates wounded. The General then continued his march to La Bruen, a strong post situated on an eminence immediately over the town of Trinité. The light infantry drove the enemy from this post after an actio of about fifteen minutes. We had two men killed and seven or eight wounded, among which were two officers. The enemy's loss was much greater. Early on the night of the 6th our troops took possession of Fort Louis (and changed its name to Fort Dundas), and Fort Bellgarde, a post that commanded the harbour of Trinité. Monf. Bellgarde, general of the army composed of people of colour, finding that we had taken possession of the forts, made a precipitate retreat towards the mountains, having previously set fire to the town of Trinité, the best part of which, together with a great quantity of stores of all kinds, was consumed; but Commodore Thompson took possession of the vessels in the harbour and road. In all these attacks the seamen (under command of Captain Salisbury) bore a part, and by their intrepidity

" Vide Appendix, page 7.

and good conduct gained the efteem as well as applaufe of the army.

On the evening of the 7th General Dundas proceeded with his brigade to the attack of Gros Morne, where he was informed General Bellgarde was ftrongly pofted in confiderable force; but on his arrival he found the forts evacuated. Gros Morne is a fituation of great importance, being ftrongly fortified, and com-manding the principal pafs between the northern and fouthern parts of the ifland, and famous for being the rendezvous of the democrats during the revolution, previous to our arrival. Befides the principal fort, there is a redoubt on either fide, about a mile diftant, commanding the road leading to the fort. A detachment of the queen's regiment and a party of the marines being left to garrifon Trinité, under command of Major Skerret, and the bat-talion of the 64th to garrifon Le Gros Morne, the remainder of the brigade marched early in the morning of the 9th inftant, and on the evening of the fame day took poffeffion of a ftrong fituation called Bruno, where there had formerly been a fort, fome of the guns of which were ftill remaining: it lies about two leagues north eaft of Fort Bourbon, and from it our army could fee the enemy in their out-pofts from that fort°. After the troops had halted for fome time, Colonel Cradock with three companies of the fecond

---

° About this time the army had nearly experienced an irreparable lofs. As General Dundas was writing in his tent, a notorious villain, of the name of Barbarofe, prefented himfelf at the door of the tent, demand-ing to fpeak with the General, who, to drive him away, called to the centinel to " bayonet the fellow; on which, in his fright, he dropped a dagger well oiled; and on being feized, proved to have been the affaffin of a French royalift.

battalion of grenadiers was ordered to advance and take poffeffion of the poft of Maltide, where a confiderable number of the ene- my were affembled with their colours flying; but on his approach they evacuated the place in hafte. Of this poft our troops had the quiet poffeffion that night, and all the next day; but in the night between the 10th and 11th they were attacked by a party of the enemy, commanded by Monf. Bellgarde, amounting to about eight hundred men, who, having crept up under cover of the canes and underwood, commenced a heavy fire on our troops, who, though rather taken by furprife, charged the enemy in their turn with fuch vigour and determined bravery, as forced them forely to repent their temerity, and retreat towards Fort Bour- bon with confiderable lofs. In this action Captain M'Ewen of the thirty-eighth regiment and feven privates were killed, and nineteen wounded. Next day a great quantity of fire arms were picked up, which the enemy had left behind them in their preci- pitate retreat. In the evening of the 11th the poft was reinforced by three companies of grenadiers and part of the fecond battalion of light infantry; but that night all was quiet. Early on the morning of the 12th the grenadiers were ordered back to Bruno, and the battalion of the fixth regiment, commanded by Major Scott, took their place at Maltide, and the wounded were fent on board the hofpital fhip.

As the bay and harbour of Fort Royal were now completely opened to our fhipping by the capture of Pigeon Ifland, the Com- mander in Chief moved forward on the 14th from La Riviere

Sallée to Bruno with the remainder of the firſt brigade, a principal part of which had, under General Preſcott, reached that place
the day before; having previouſly concerted the attack of St. Pierré
with General Dundas, that general marched on the evening of
the 13th from Bruno with the ſecond battalion of grenadiers, the
thirty-third and fortieth light companies, and the ſixty-fifth regiment, to Gros Morne, where he halted that night, and early on
the 14th marched to Trinité; from whence he diſpatched a ſloop
with the packs and blankets of his army round towards la Baſſe
Pointe, in order to expedite his march toward St. Pierre, the
capital of the iſland, the capture of which was now his object.
From Gros Morne General Dundas had detached Colonel Campbell through the woods by Bois le Buc with the ſecond battalion
of light infantry and ſixty-fifth regiment to Montigné. At five
o'clock in the evening of the 14th General Dundas marched from
Trinité (being joined by a company of the ſecond or queen's regiment, commanded by the Honourable Captain Ramſay): after
marching all night he halted for three hours; and ſoon after day-
break on the morning of the 15th, having paſſed the river Capot,
arrived at the heights of Calbaſs, after a march of thirty miles
over a rough mountainous country. The fatigue of ſuch a march
in a tropical climate can only be conceived by thoſe who have experienced it: haraſſed and worn down, it was neceſſary to give the
troops ſome reſt before they attempted to aſcend the ſteep and
craggy mountain, over the top of which was their road, commanded by a battery, where the enemy appeared in great force,

with their colours flying. The spirit of our soldiers however over-
came all difficulties, and they ascended the heights with such
alacrity, that the enemy, alarmed at their determined conduct,
evacuated the fort (fortunately for our men), without making any
resistance; as, by the time they reached the summit of the mountain, they were so exhausted, that a steady opposition might have
proved fatal to them. From hence (the post having previously
been destroyed by the enemy, who had broken the guns and scat-
tered the ammunition) General Dundas proceeded about four
miles further, to a place called Morne Rouge: here he halted,
and shortly after saw Colonel Campbell at Post au Pin, half a mile
short of Montigné, under a heavy fire from five or six hundred of
the enemy, strongly posted. General Dundas instantly pushed
forward his advanced guard, under command of the Hon. Captain
Ramsay, who gained the summit by extraordinary exertions, fired
on the enemy, at that time engaged with Colonel Campbell, and
silenced their fire; and, when joined by the second battalion of
grenadiers, took possession of Montigné, where he was reinforced
by two companies of grenadiers. The major general took post
himself on Morne Rouge, and visiting Colonel Campbell's column,
found he had been attacked at half past nine o clock in the morning, and the enemy being within twenty yards of the fortieth
light company, at the head of which he was, had charged them
with bayonets, when, to the great grief of the whole army, he
fell by a ball through his head from the musket of a mulatto, who
had concealed himself behind a bush till the Colonel came close

up to it. Colonel Campbell was a man high in eſtimation as a
military character, and no leſs reſpected for his private worth,
being ſincere in his friendſhips and ſteady in his attachments.
When General Dundas arrived at Morne Rouge, the enemy were
on their march to re-attack our troops; but the appearance of our
grenadiers ſo near them, cauſed them to relinquiſh their plan at
that time: but in the evening of the ſame day the General obſerved bodies of the enemy moving towards his front at Morne
Rouge, and forming under a ſmall redoubt near that poſt. The
thirty-third, thirty-fourth, and forty-fourth companies of grenadiers, with a field piece, and Captain Whitworth of the artillery
(the whole under the command of Major Forbes), were ordered
to advance, when a ſmart engagement commenced. The enemy
were covered by a briſk fire from two field pieces on Morne Bellvieu, a ſtrongly ſituated battery immediately in their rear. The
action continued for about half an hour, when the enemy gave
way, and during the night abandoned the fort, leaving two field
pieces behind them. From the number of graves obſerved the
following day (corroborated by the accounts of ſome priſoners),
their loſs muſt have been conſiderable; ours conſiſted of one
officer (Lieutenant Keating of the thirty-third regiment) and two
privates wounded, and one private killed.—At two o'clock the
following morning the ſixteenth, thirty-fifth, and fifty-fifth companies of grenadiers were ordered to advance and ſtorm the battery upon Morne Bellvieu, and were to be ſupported (if neceſſary)
by the ninth and ſixty-fifth companies. All their flints were taken

out, the bayonet alone to be the foldier's defence. However, the
enemy had been fo roughly handled the day before, that they
thought fit to decamp during the night, and our troops took poffeffion of the fort without any oppofition. Our army had now
arrived within two leagues of St. Pierre, from whence by day-break
the enemy fent a flag of truce, requiring three days to confider of
a capitulation; to which General Dundas returned an anfwer, that
inftead of three days, he would allow them only three hours; and
if they did not furrender within that time, he would advance
againft the town. The fifty-fifth company of grenadiers being
left in poffeffion of Bellvieu, the remainder of the battalion moved
on towards St. Pierré. In the mean time the Admiral, Sir John
Jervis, to co-operate with the land forces under General Dundas,
had ordered the following fhips to fail for the bay of St. Pierre,
the Afia, Veteran, Santa Margarita, Blonde, Rattlefnake, Zebra,
and Nautilus, with the Vefuvius bomb. On board of this fleet
Colonel Symes had embarked with three light companies, and
Major Maitland with a detachment of the fiftieth regiment; Colonel Myers with five companies of the firft battalion of grenadiers, and five companies of the third battalion of light infantry,
(for the fame purpofe of co-operating with General Dundas) had
marched from Camp la Cofte towards Trinité.

The fleet on their arrival in the bay prepared for inftant operation. Colonel Symes, with the troops and feamen who were to
land with him, had, previous to their entering the bay, embarked
on board of the Zebra and Nautilus floops, and fome other vef-

fels, which, being fmall, could get nearer the fhore, thereby rendering the debarkation of the troops much lefs difficult.

In the evening of Feb. 16th they began to work towards the north part of the bay, beyond the Jefuits' College, the other men of war ftanding towards the town to cover them. About eleven o'clock the veffels with troops and feamen on board were under a crofs fire from two batteries of red hot fhot, which happily did them no damage, though they fell round and near them. Captain Harvey in the Santa Margarita, perceiving the troops were likely to be much annoyed, went clofe under the guns of the moft confiderable of the two batteries, which he filenced; and about four in the morning of the 17th the troops and feamen made good their landing, and found that the enemy had left the other battery. During the night the Vefuvius bomb did much execution with her fhells, many of them falling in the town, to which it fet fire in fome places: the fire however was foon extinguifhed. The batteries in the town and on the adjacent hills kept up a conftant fire of fhot and fhells on the men of war, as they advanced towards the town, which was returned with great fpirit. The Santa Margarita was ftruck with a fhell, which fortunately neither fired her, nor did any confiderable damage. Colonel Symes on landing advanced with the troops towards St. Pierre, which the enemy evacuated on his approach, leaving their guns primed and loaded, and their colours flying, which were hauled down by our people, and the Britifh union hoifted. About ten the whole of the troops and feamen had marched into the town. No man was fuffered to quit his ranks, nor was the leaſt injury done to any of the inhabitants, who, with the women and children, ſat at their doors and windows to ſee our army march in, the ſame as when troops paſs through a town in England. While our men were drawn up in the market place, a flag of truce came in from General Dundas, who with his army was on the hills near the town, and was on his march to attack it. This flag was in anſwer to one ſent by the enemy to him, offering to capitulate. The officer who brought the flag was agreeably ſurpriſed to find on his entering the town that it was already in the poſſeſſion of his countrymen. In the evening General Dundas with the army marched in; and having taken poſſeſſion of the government-houſe, he inſtantly eſtabliſhed quiet and good order in the town. As our troops marched into St. Pierre a drummer was diſcovered in the act of plundering one of the peaceable inhabitants, for which he was inſtantly hung up at the gate of ·the Jeſuits' College, by order of the provoſt marſhal. In the evening the ſeamen embarked on board their reſpective ſhips. The men of war having anchored in the bay, were buſily employed in taking an account of and unbending the ſails of the different ſhips in the harbour. Unfortunately at day-break of this morning, when the town ſurrendered, a ſchooner got out of the ſouth ſide of the bay, in which it was reported there was a conſiderable quantity of money and ſome people of diſtinction. She paſſed within gun-ſhot of the Santa Margarita, who (for ſome reaſon or other) did not fire at her to bring her to. The next morning the Santa Margarita ſailed to Fort Royal bay with Monſ.

Au Cane[p], the mayor of St. Pierre, and Abbé Maunier, the vicar general of the ifland, and other prifoners.

St. Pierre is a long handfome town, fituated on the fhore of an open bay, and flanked by a ftrong battery at either end; alfo defended by two redoubts on the hills which overhang the town. The furrounding country rifes in a fucceffion of hills beautifully variegated with woods and fugar plantations; and near the town are fome fine gardens, which before the revolution had been kept up in a fuperior ftile of elegance and convenience. Each ftreet of this beautiful town is watered by a clear ftream from the mountains, running rapidly down the middle, which adds greatly to the health as well as convenience of the place. The ftreets in general are narrow and rough paved, but very regular; the houfes are built of a fine ftone like free-ftone, the lower apartments of which were in general handfomely, and fometimes fuperbly, furnifhed.

There are two convents of nuns, one dedicated to St. Urfuline, the other called Les Blancs. The Urfuline convent has very beautiful gardens, fituated at the declivity of a hill, which rifes immediately behind the town: it was in a wretched ftate when we took it, the poor nuns having been deprived of their revenues by the revolutionifts. Near this convent is a neat church,

[p] On our firft arrival at the ifland of Martinique, the Commanders in Chief difpatched Captain Mafon (aid de camp to the General) bearing a flag of truce, with a fummons to the town of St. Pierre. Au Cane, the mayor, met him on the quay on horfeback, attended by a numerous body of armed men, with a field piece, &c. and inftead of reading the letter and fummons, difmiffed him rudely with threats.

whofe high altar, as well as pavement, is of good marble. Not far from the church is the opera houfe, which, from its high roof, is a very confpicuous object. Towards the fouth end of the town is the church of Notre Dame de bon Porte du Mouillage (of which Pere Maunier, one of the chiefs of the revolution, was curé). It is a handfome building: round the grand altar (which is of polifhed and well fculptured marble) are feveral tolerable paintings of faints and the Virgin Mary, as large as life. Over the bridge, at the north end of the town, is another large church, and feveral others, fmall and mean in their outward appearance and infide decorations. I was informed that moft of thefe churches were well endowed before the revolution, and the religious houfes were amply provided for, as is the cafe in all parts of the new world where the Roman Catholic religion is profeffed.

At the northern extremity of St. Pierre is a fpacious handfome houfe, with good offices, ftables, and gardens, which formerly belonged to the Jefuits, in whofe diftrict the town and furrounding country is fituated. The Capuchins and Dominicans had the two other parts of the ifland.—The government-houfe, which on our taking it was inhabited by Au Cane, the mayor, is conveniently fituated near the centre of the town, and was formed for the refidence of the chief magiftrate or governor of the ifland. The rooms are large and lofty, and there is a good garden at the back of the houfe, in which, amongft a variety of fruit trees, was a fine bread-fruit tree: how it came there, I could not learn, unlefs fome French fhips had paid a vifit to the iflands in the South Sea, for the fame purpofe that our fhips of late have made that voyage; but then I think more of the trees would have been feen in this and the neighbouring French iflands.—Towards the fouthern end of the town is a large and commodious hofpital, which had good revenues attached to it, and was well regulated and attended. This we found of infinite ufe for our fick and wounded, who were far better provided for here than they could be in the hofpital fhips, or with the army.

CHAPTER VI.

THE ENEMY RETIRE INTO FORT BOURBON AND FORT LOUIS....
THE ADMIRAL ATTACKS FORT LOUIS WITH THE BOMB-KETCH
AND GUN-BOATS....CAMP OF SEAMEN FORMED AT POINT
NEGRO....A WHARF BUILT IN THE CUL DE SAC DE COHEE,
STORES AND AMMUNITION LANDED THERE....GENERAL
BELLGARDE ATTEMPTS TO CUT OFF THE COMMUNICATION
BETWEEN THE ARMY AND NAVY, BUT IS BEATEN, AND HIS
CAMP ON SOURIER TAKEN....HEAD-QUARTERS ESTABLISHED
ON SOURIER....GENERAL ROCHAMBEAU SENDS AN AID DE
CAMP TO THE COMMANDERS IN CHIEF....THE NAVY MAKE
A ROAD, AND DRAG THE GUNS TO THE HEIGHTS OF SOURIER.

Sᴛ. Pierre being now captured[q], the enemy's ſtrength was con-
centrated in one point at Forts Louis and Bourbon: the latter is
a work of late date, being built under the directions of the preſent Marquis de Bouillé, and is a well planned as well as ſtrongly
ſituated fortification; but in this mountainous country it is hardly

---

[q] Information having arrived that ſome of the enemy had retired from St. Pierre to a five-gun battery on
that part of the iſland, Major Manningham was diſpatched with a ſtrong detachment in flat-boats, under the
protection of the Zebra ſloop of war, and was completely ſucceſsful in driving them from thence.

poffible to find any fpot that may not be commanded by fome neighbouring height, unlefs on the tops of the mountains, where it would be difficult to procure water and provifions fufficient for the fubfiftence of an army during a fiege of any length. The town of Fort Royal is fituated on a flat and fwampy ground, at the foot of the hill on which is Fort Bourbon; and Fort Louis, the ancient ftrong-hold of this ifland, is on a neck of land running into the fea, and forms one fide of the Carénage, an excellent harbour for fhipping of all kinds.—The Admiral, from the day he anchored in Fort Royal Bay, began a heavy cannonade on Fort Louis. The Vefuvius bomb, commanded by Captain Sawyer, and under the direction of Captain Suckling of the artillery, threw fhells into the fort from an eighteen-inch and twelve-inch mortar with great effect; and as foon as the evening fhut in, the gun-boats, attended by feveral row-boats from the fhips in the fleet (to affift in cafe of their being funk by the enemy's fhot) moved towards the mouth of the Carénage, and commenced a brifk fire on the fort, which was generally returned with equal fpirit; but, from the fmallnefs of the object, and frequently fhifting their fituation, they were lefs often hit than could have been expected, confidering that they conftantly were within the range of grape-fhot, which fell in fhowers round them. Towards day-break they returned to their refpective fhips.—In the night of February 15th, the fecond and third companies of feamen, under the command of Lieutenants Miln and Ogle, left the Boyne; and, with other feamen from the fleet, the whole under command of Captain Rogers of the Quebec, landed at Cas Navire, and (occupying the pofts that the troops under Colonel Myers had that day quitted, to affift in the attack on St. Pierre) formed a camp near Point Negro.—Our fhipping having now, by the capture of Pigeon Ifland, free ingrefs to Fort Royal bay, moft of the tranfports and ftore-fhips, under convoy of his majefty's fhips Santa Margarita, Solebay, Nautilus, &c. got up into the Cul de fac de Cohée, an harbour at the north-eaft end of the bay, from whence they had a communication with the army under Sir Charles Grey, and where they built a wharf to land provifions and ftores; and a chain of pofts was eftablifhed from thence to the heights of Bruno, on which duty the fifteenth and twentieth regiments were employed.—On February 18th in the morning, General Bellgarde moved with nearly his whole force from his camp on the heights of Sourier, to attack the landing-place in the Cul de fac de Cohée, and by that means to cut off the communication between the army and the fleet. Sir Charles Grey, with that quicknefs of perception that has rendered him fo often ufeful to his country, inftantly perceived his defign, and without lofs of time ordered the grenadiers, under the command of Colonel Buckridge, and the light infantry, under that of Colonel Coote, to advance with the utmoft expedition, and attack Monf. Bellgarde's camp at Sourier; and detached a ftrong corps from the heights of Bruno to fupport them. They began their attack on the enemy in the wood; and having driven them from thence, began to mount the rugged and almoft inacceffible fides of the hill on which Sourier was fituated. The troops gallantly

H

forced their way through every obftruction, and mounted the heights under a heavy. fire from the retreating enemy, whom they fairly drove up the precipice, and gained the heights, where they found an excellent dinner (provided for Bellgarde and his people) to refrefh them after their fatigue. Our lofs in this affair' was by no means fo great as might have been expected, confidering the length of ground, and the many difadvantages under which our troops engaged. While this was doing, General Sir Charles Grey cannonaded Bellgarde from the camp at Bruno, whofe troops foon retired in confufion to their late camp at Sourier, which they found occupied by the Britifh grenadiers, who turned their own guns on them (confifting of three brafs field pieces), and drove them in confufion under the walls of Fort Bourbon. Our foldiers could not now be reftrained, but with an impetuofity that General Prefcott could not for the moment prevent, advanced fo near the fort, that the enemy opening a heavy fire of grape fhot on them, obliged them at length to retire with fome lofs to their new acquifition on Sourier, a poft which Sir Charles Grey had intended to have attacked the following day, as being abfolutely neceffary to enable him to carry on his plan of attack againft Fort Bourbon, and which the temerity of Bellgarde had thus put into his hands a day fooner.—The whole bufinefs of this action was conducted in fuch a manner, that each individual concerned par-

' According to the beft account I could collect, ten killed and forty-four wounded.—I muft here beg the reader will pardon the inaccuracy of my account of the killed and wounded in this and the other actions that took place. Though I have made every poffible inquiry, I have not been able to meet with the regular returns, which muft have been given in to the adjutant general's office at Martinique.

took of the glory of it; and when confidered as to its utility, it was perhaps one of the moft fortunate, as well as the beft conducted, enterprifes that happened throughout the campaign The day after this event General Rochambeau, who commanded in Fort Bourbon, fent an aid de camp on board the Boyne, who went thence with Captain Grey to the Commander in Chief at head quarters. The terms of capitulation that he brought were, that the whole ifland fhould be delivered to the Englifh on condition that, in cafe Louis the Seventeenth fhould ever come to the throne, it fhould be reftored to him; if not, and the republic fhould be eftablifhed, it fhould be given up to that government. The Commander in Chief returned for anfwer, ' that he came ex-‹ prefsly to take this ifland for his Britannic Majefty; and that he ‹ hoped to take all the French iflands in this quarter on the fame ‹ account.'—The troops now pitched their tents, and formed their camp on Sourier. General Prefcott's quarters were in this camp, where he commanded; and Sir Charles Grey eftablifhed his head quarters at a fmall diftance in the rear.—General Dundas having arranged every thing relative to the government of St. Pierre, left Colonel Myers of the fifteenth regiment with the battalions of the fifty-eighth and fixty-fifth regiments to garrifon that town, and on February 20th embarked with the grenadiers on board the Veteran for Fort Royal Bay. The morning following they difembarked in the Cul de fac de Cohée, and marched directly to head quarters at Sourier, where they pitched their tents, and with regret parted from General Dundas, their commander hitherto,

who went to Camp la Cofte to take the command of the light infantry.—The artillery, artificers, and engineers, were now bufily
employed in landing ftores and ammunition preparatory to the
formation of the batteries neceffary for the fiege; in which bufinefs they received great affiftance from a body of feamen landed
for that purpofe: three hundred of thefe brave fellows were
landed at the wharf in the Cul de fac Cohée from his majefty's
fhips Santa Margarita, Captain Harvey, with his Lieutenants
Woolley and Harrifon; the Solebay, Captain Kelly, with Lieutenants Carthew and Schomberg; and Nautilus floop, Captain
Carpenter; with Lieutenant Bennet, Lieutenant Collins, and a
party of marines, from the Santa Margarita. They inftantly began to proceed with a twenty-four pounder and two fix pounders[s] towards Sourier. They halted with the twenty-four pounder
that evening on the fide of the road between Fort Royal and the
town of Lamantin, as they were obliged to cut a road through a
thick wood for nearly a mile. The next day they completed the
road, and alfo made a fort of bridge, or rather paffage, acrofs a
river, which at times was of confiderable depth, though fortunately there was now only four feet water in it. This they effected by filling it up with large ftones and branches of trees, and
then they proceeded with the twenty-four pounder and two eight-
inch howitzers, which they left that night in charge of a piquet
from the poft above mentioned. On the third day they, to the

_____

[s] The two fix-pounders were to ftrengthen the poft that commanded the road to Fort Royal by Dillon's houfe.

astonishment of the whole army, got a twenty-four pounder to the heights of Sourier before the night shut in, and two howitzers within a mile of it; and to add to the difficulty, a considerable part of that day was employed in levelling the banks of the river that runs by Dillon's plantation, and making it fordable, by removing immense stones and fragments of rock. On the fourth day (notwithstanding they were obliged to employ a considerable party in making the road more complete) they got the two howitzers above mentioned, and two more twenty-four pounders, to the heights of Sourier. The distance from the wharf to those heights is near five miles; and when we consider that the road was to be formed for near four miles of the way, one of which was through a very thick wood, and that, as they approached the heights of Sourier, for near a mile the road was so steep, that a loaded mule could not walk directly up it, it seems scarce credible that so small a number as three hundred men should be able to have undergone such severe fatigue, considering the climate and the nature of the soil, which was a very stiff clay, intermixed with large rock stones.—A few days after, a reinforcement of seamen was landed from the Veteran, Captain Nugent, with Lieutenants Leaf and Whitlock, and the Winchelsea, Lord Viscount Garlies, with his Lieutenants Dixon and Watson; also Lieutenant Treminere of the marines, with a sergeant's party. They took post by the side of the road leading from Lamantin to Fort Royal, where the first twenty-four pounder was halted.—The first party of seamen took post on the banks of the river running past Dillon's plantation, at the foot of the heights of Sourier. But the Veteran being wanted for other fervice, in the courfe of the week one hundred and fifty men were reimbarked on board her, and the Winchelfea's crew joined the former party. The compliments paid the feamen in general orders for their fpirited conduct, is a convincing proof that they never once relaxed from their firft exertions from the beginning of the fiege to the furrender of Fort Bourbon, a period of five weeks. Indeed their aftonifhing exertions were almoft beyond probability: after rain (which in this climate is frequent) the fteep parts of the road were fo flippery, that a man even with the greateft care would frequently flip back ten and fometimes twenty feet at a time: but fo determined were the honeft tars not to fail in what they undertook, that when once they fet out with their gun after a heavy rain, and they found it impoffible to keep their feet, they have crawled up as they dragged the twenty-four pounder, and kept themfelves from fliding back by fticking their fingers in the ground. But among the many compliments paid the feamen, none pleafed them fo much as having a battery appointed folely for them, where they ufed to relieve one another by turns, without even an additional allowance of grog as an encouragement. Sir Charles Grey paid

᠁ One day, when the Commander in Chief met them on the road, they (being ignorant that a battery was appointed for them to ferve in) furrounded the General, and offered him their fervices, fwearing they thought it d——d hard to have all work and no fighting; and hoped his Honour would let them have fome fhare in it. The General, with that kindnefs which won the hearts of all that had the happinefs to ferve under him, faid, "Well, my lads, you fhall have a battery to yourfelves." On which, having faluted him with three hearty cheers, the honeft fellows went readily to their work again.

the higheſt compliments to the zeal and ability with which the Admiral ſeconded all his plans. Indeed there never was an inſtance in which two commanders carried on a buſineſs of ſuch importance ſo unalloyed by the leaſt difference in opinion, or jealouſy of command: each ſtrove to prove his readineſs to aſſiſt his friend and colleague; of courſe every thing ſucceeded, and was carried on with a promptneſs of execution that ſeldom has been equalled, never exceeded.

CHAPTER VII.

FORTS BOURBON AND LOUIS CLOSELY INVESTED.... BATTERIES
ON THE FIRST PARALLEL ERECTED.... THE SEAMEN EMPLOY-
ED IN GETTING GUNS TO THE BATTERIES ON THE WEST
SIDE.... A DANGEROUS PASS DESCRIBED.... CAPTAIN MILN'
MORTALLY WOUNDED; HE DIES; HIS CHARACTER.... BELL-
GARDE DELIVERS HIMSELF AND ARMY INTO THE HANDS OF
SIR CHARLES GREY.... HIS ROYAL HIGHNESS PRINCE ED-
WARD ARRIVES, AND TAKES A COMMAND.... BATTERIES
OPENED AGAINST FORT BOURBON... LIEUTENANT BOWEN'S
SPIRITED CONDUCT.... FORT LOUIS TAKEN BY STORM....
CAPTAIN FAULKNOR'S GALLANT CONDUCT.... FORT BOURBON
SURRENDERS.

FROM the 20th of February Forts Bourbon and Louis, with the
town of Fort Royal, were completely invested, and the General
was busily employed in erecting batteries on his first parallel.
On the north-east side the army under General Prescott broke
ground on the 25th of February, and on the west side towards La Coste (where Sir Charles Gordon commanded, Prince
Edward not having as yet arrived from Canada) fascine batte-

I

ries for mortars and cannon were erecting with every poſſible expedition. In this buſineſs the ſeamen, who formed a camp at Point Negro under Captain Joſias Rogers of the Quebec, eminently diſtinguiſhed themſelves; and though the roads were not quite ſo bad as on the Sourier ſide, yet they had many ſevere difficulties to encounter, that rendered dragging the mortars and heavy ordnance to the batteries fatiguing and hazardous in a great degree. Part of the way which they were obliged to go was in ſight of Fort Bourbon; ſoon after which they deſcended into a hollow way or ravine, where a rivulet invited them to refreſh themſelves, and it was with difficulty their officers could prevent them from ſlaking their thirſt at this ſtream, which croſſed them at a time when the fatigue and heat they ſuſtained rendered the temptation almoſt irreſiſtible, eſpecially to men fearleſs of danger, and thoughtleſs to a proverb. No ſooner did they begin to deſcend into this ravine, than the enemy threw their ſhells with ſuch judgment, that they frequently fell at the moment our people were paſſing the rivulet. It was in the afternoon of the 22d of February that Lieutenant James Miln of the Boyne was proceeding with his company of ſeamen to relieve thoſe who had been the fore-part of the day at work on one of the advanced batteries, and having been obſerved on his march by the enemy in Fort Bourbon, they as uſual began to fire their mortars into the ravine; Mr. Miln, who, added to the greateſt courage, poſſeſſed much prudence, was hurrying his men through this dangerous paſs, and was in the act of calling to two men who were drinking at the rivulet (the reſt of his company having paſſed on), when a ſhell burſt near him, carried off one of his legs, and ſhattered the other in a dreadful manner. At the ſame time one of the men, who had loitered, loſt a leg. In this dreadful ſituation he was carried two miles to Sir Charles Gordon's camp, before his wounds could be bound up, and from thence to his own quarters at Point Negro, where he ſuffered amputation of one leg. The next day the ſurgeon general of the navy went to him from the Boyne, and finding his ſituation dangerous in the extreme, having no better place than the ground, in an open ſugar-houſe, part of which was the head quarters of the naval officers, and being within range of the enemy's guns, which frequently threw their ſhot and ſhells over him, he was conveyed to the royal hoſpital at St. Pierre; but from the loſs of blood he had ſuſtained, and the nature of the climate, he was ſeized with the lock jaw, of which he died on Sunday the 9th of March, and the next day was buried in the garden of the hoſpital with the honours of war, together with Lieutenants Spencer and Roſehill[u] of the Beaulieu, and Lieutenant Smith of the fifty-eighth regiment. The burial ſervice was performed by the Chaplain[v] of the Boyne, and attended by Colonel Myers, commandant of St. Pierre, Captain Saliſbury of the Beaulieu, and the other naval and military officers, and the principal Engliſh gentlemen who were in that

[u] The Admiral had lately promoted Mr. Roſehill to the rank of Lieutenant for his ſpirited behaviour at Trinité.

[v] Who this day performed the funeral ſervice over thirteen people belonging to the army and navy.

town. The Admiral, who always diftinguifhed merit, and rewarded it when in his power, had promoted Mr. Miln ^w to the command of the Avenger floop, late Marfeillois, taken at St. Pierre.

Bellgarde found it in vain to attempt any thing further, after his laft fhameful defeat; and being with his black army fhut out of Fort Bourbon by General Rochambeau (who, when he retreated after the lofs of his camp on Sourier under cover of the fire of that fort, fhut the gates againft him), he now determined to make the beft bargain he could for himfelf; and accordingly on the 25th of February fent a meffage to Sir Charles Grey, offering to give up his army, on condition that himfelf, and certain others that he named, fhould be permitted to go to America; which requeft the Commander in Chief complied with; and on the 4th of March, Bellgarde, with his fecretary, a white man, by whofe councils he had always been guided, and eight people of colour,

w As it was my lot to be much in the fociety of this excellent young man, having from the time we arrived in the Weft Indies enjoyed his friendfhip, and on feveral occafions accompanied him on fervice, afterwards attending him from the camp at Point Negro to the hofpital at St. Pierre, and remaining with him at intervals till the time of his death: thefe circumftances will, I truft, plead my excufe for detaining the reader from more important events of the campaign while I pay the tribute of refpect to the memory of my gallant but ill-fated friend. Mr. James Miln was a native of Arbroath in Scotland, and after ferving for near thirteen years with credit in the navy, was promoted to a lieutenancy on board the Blanche frigate by Admiral Sir John Laforey, and was afterwards taken on board the Boyne as fifth lieutenant by Sir John Jervis on his arrival at Barbadoes. His general good conduct as a man and officer foon attracted the notice of the naval Commander in Chief (than whom no man is more quick fighted to difcern merit, and happy to reward it). By him no doubt he would have been much employed on the moft active fervice, had not that melancholy event taken place, which deprived the fervice of a good and brave officer, and left me only the fad tafk of deploring, while I commemorate the death of a friend, from the excellency of whofe heart and underftanding I was in hopes of reaping future entertainment and improvement.

failed in a fchooner for America, whither he had taken the precaution at various times to forward a quantity of wealth againft
any change of circumftances fhould make fuch a retreat defirable[x].

On Tuefday the 4th of March his Royal Highnefs Prince Edward arrived at this ifland, and was received with a royal falute
from the fleet.   Immediately he took the command of that brigade of the army encamped on the Cas Navire fide, and at **La
Cofte**, which had hitherto been under the direction of Sir Charles
Gordon[y].—Intelligence having reached the Commander in Chief
that a number of brigands, compofed of fome runaways from
Bellgarde's army, and other wretches, had committed many de-
predations and murders, pillaging and burning houfes and villages
in feveral parts of the ifland; he difpatched a detachment of the
fifteenth regiment, commanded by Lord Sinclair, with a party of
the Prince of Wales's light dragoons, commanded by Lieut. Shadwell, and conducted by Captain Cunningham (one of his Excellency's aid de camps), who furprifed one hundred and fifty of thefe
people in the act of burning and plundering the village of Francois[z].   At the firft charge the enemy were routed, thirty-fix of
them, with their chief (who was cut down by a dragoon), were
killed, and four taken prifoners, who were inftantly hung up, to

[x] Since writing of this, news has arrived from the Weft Indies of the capture of a fhip belonging to
Victor Hughes (the prefent republican tyrant of Guadaloupe) loaded with wealth amaffed by this plunderer
to the amount of half a million fterling.   Such has been the general conduct of the French Commanders,
while ours have been vilified for claiming even the legal bounty for their fuffering and exhaufted followers.

[y] See Appendix, page 24.   [z] See Appendix, page 25.

deter others from fuch infamous acts as had been committed by thefe mifcreants.—Every preparation was now made for opening our batteries againft Fort Bourbon, which were conftructed only about eight hundred paces from the fort, and about fix hundred in front of our own lines. Thefe batteries would have been conftructed much fooner, but, owing to the heavy rains that fell almoft conftantly, and which, at this feafon of the year, were unufual, the works had been greatly retarded, and the difficulties encreafed. On the morning of the 6th of March, every thing being ready for a heavy cannonade, Sir Charles Grey fent a flag of truce with a fummons to the garrifon to furrender, which was refufed by General Rochambeau. Accordingly, at day-break on the 7th (the gun-boats having as ufual attacked Fort Louis during the night) mortars, howitzers, and great guns, opened from five batteries at the fame inftant, keeping up an inceffant fire on the fort and advanced redoubt the whole of that day and the night, from each of which it was returned with equal fury. All the following day the fame fpirited attack and defence was continued. On the 9th the enemy made a fortie fron the fort, and attacked the advanced picquet from the camp at La Cofte, compofed of part of the third battalion of light infantry, and fome failors under command of Captain Faulknor of the Zebra. After an engagement of fome length the enemy gave way, and were imprudently followed by our troops under the guns of the fort; by this excefs of ardour we loft fome men, while the enemy fuffered but little. The gun-boats and Vefuvius now kept up a

conftant fire from Fort Royal Bay: in the former two feamen
were killed by grape, and part of the head of the bomb ketch
was fhot away. On the 13th a melancholy accident occurred in
one of our batteries, which was formed and manned entirely by
feamen. Captain Faulknor of the Zebra, who commanded in it,
being provoked by the interference of an officer of artillery in the
works which one of the feamen of the Afia was employed in, and
the failor not obeying him with alacrity, was provoked to ftrike
him with his fword, which unfortunately wounded him mortally,
and he died in a few minutes. Captain Faulknor was acquitted
by the court martial that was inftantly fummoned by the Admiral
to inveftigate the matter; and the circumftance of its happening
in the heat of action, when the leaft difobedience of orders in-
volves the moft fatal confequences, as well, as that it appeared there
was no premeditated intention of killing the unfortunate man,
but was a blow given from the impulfe of momentary paffion;
the fentence was confirmed and approved.—From this time the
fiege was carried on with unremitted exertion by night and day;
fhot and fhells were conftantly flying, and new batteries daily conftructed; fo that our advanced batteries were at length brought
within five hundred yards of the fort, and not more than two hundred from the redoubt: the latter indeed was fo battered, that it
might with eafe have been ftormed; but the General knew that
a mine which communicated from the fort would involve in certain deftruction all who attempted fo defperate an action; and
therefore preferred the more fure means of fuccefs, by regular

and methodical approaches. On Monday the 17th of March two new batteries opened on Fort Louis from Point Carriere, a neck of land that forms the fouth-weft fide of the Carénage, and not more than two hundred yards acrofs the mouth of that harbour to the walls of the fort; one of thefe was commanded by Captain Riou[a] of the Rofe.—The French had a fine frigate called the Bienvenu, which was anchored in the centre of the Carénage, on board of which it was reported a number of Englifh prifoners were confined, and were confequently expofed to the fire of our batteries. Lieut. Bowen of the Boyne formed a refolution to extricate his countrymen from their perilous fituation; and having obtained the Admiral's permiffion, and approbation of his plan, at noon he boldly pufhed into the harbour from Point Carriere, where he had collected his boats deftined for the enterprife, well manned by tried and determined feamen. The inftant he appeared round the point, the enemy prepared to give him a warm reception. The walls of Fort Louis were covered in an inftant with troops, which kept up an inceffant fire of mufquetry on him; at the fame time the frigate endeavoured to keep him off, by plying both her great guns and fmall arms; but at length, intimidated by the boldnefs of the attempt, they fled from their quarters, and Mr. Bowen at the head of his men boarded the frigate, and took the captain, officers, and crew of her prifoners without refiftance. All this time the enemy in the fort continued to pour vollies of

[a] The fame officer who diftinguifhed himfelf by his gallantry in faving his Majefty's fhip the Guardian at the Cape of Good Hope in the year 1789. See Gent. Mag. vol. lx. page 465.

grape and mufketry on the frigate, which was returned with great fpirit by the Britifh feamen, who now turned their own guns upon them, and would have brought her out of the harbour, but the fails being all unbent, it was impoffible in fuch a fituation to bend them: the tri-coloured flag, which was faftened to the gaff of the mizen, they were not able to ftrike, though a failor had the audacity to go aloft for that purpofe, fcorning the mufketry of the enemy. Mr. Bowen, feeing no chance of getting the fhip out of the harbour, and finding that the Englifh prifoners were in another veffel further up, from whence it was rendered impof-fible to releafe them, contented himfelf with fecuring the officers and crew of the frigate, whom he brought off, in fpite of every effort made by the republicans to prevent him. As the bullets were flying thick around him, he fuffered the Frenchmen to lie down in the bottom of the boats, that they might not be killed by their own countrymen; a very different conduct from what they had obferved to our people who were in the fame fituation[b]. In this bufinefs he loft only three men killed, and four or five wounded. The fuccefs of this enterprife gave the Commanders in Chief confidence, that a fpirited attack by land and fea on Fort Louis would fucceed. Accordingly the Admiral ordered a num-ber of bamboos of thirty feet long to be cut and made into fcal-ing ladders, connected with ftrong line. The gun-boats and row-boats were collected in the bay round the Point Carriere, and the failors' camp at Point Negro, with Prince Edward's camp at La

[b] See Appendix, pages 26 and 27.

Cofte and Cas Navire, held themfelves in readinefs to co-operate in the grand attack. The navy to be employed in this bufinefs was under the immediate direction of Commodore Thompfon. On Thurfday the 20th of March, before day-break, the third battalion of grenadiers, commanded by Lieutenant Colonel Buckridge, and the firft battalion of light infantry, commanded by Lieutenant Colonel Coote, marched by the hill on which Fort Bourbon is fituated from the camp on Sourier, unperceived by the enemy, and took a pofition that gave them the command of the bridge that connected the town of Fort Royal to the road leading up to that fort, the batteries on the fecond parallel being ready, thofe on Morne Tortenfon and Point Carriere kept up a well-directed and heavy fire on Fort Louis, and all the other batteries cannonaded Fort Bourbon during the whole of the day and night of the 19th inftant, and on the morning alfo, till about ten o'clock, when the Afia of 64 guns, Captain Browne, and the Zebra floop of 16 guns, Captain R. Faulknor, got under way. The Zebra led in towards the mouth of the harbour, receiving the fire of grape and round, without returning a fhot: the Afia had got within the range of grape fhot, when, to the furprife of every body, fhe wore and made fail from the fort[c]. The Admiral, Sir John Jervis, had previoufly made the fignal for the reft of the fleet to be ready to fecond the attempt of thefe two fhips, by loofing the topfails of the Boyne, and lying at fingle anchor ready

[c] Monfieur de Tourelles, the ancient lieutenant of the fort, either through fear, ignorance, or treachery, refufed to run the fhip in under pretence of fhoals.

to flip and run in; on perceiving the Afia was foiled in her attempt, and fuppofing, as fhe was under a heavy fire from the fort, that either Captain Browne was killed, or that fome other defperate accident had happened, he inftantly difpatched Captain George Grey of the Boyne to take the command of the Afia, and if he could not get in, to run her aground under the walls of the fort. Captain Grey foon returned, and brought the pleafing intelligence that not a man was hurt on board of the Afia. She then ftood in again, and again put about, when near the mouth of the harbour, and failed from it. Captain Faulknor, feeing that he ftood no chance of being feconded by the Afia, and being all this time under a dreadful fire from Fort Louis, boldly pufhed in towards that fort, ftill referving his fire till he came clofe to the walls of it; and then running his fhip aground, plying his fmall arms and great guns, he drove the enemy from thence, and leaping into a boat, fcaled the ramparts. Seeing the Zebra go in, all the boats with fcaling ladders, attended by the gun-boats, feemed to fly towards the fcene of action. Thofe from Point Carriere mounted the walls near where Captain Faulknor had fo gallantly run his fhip, and feconding him, drove the enemy out of the fort, hauled down the republican flag, and hoifted the Britifh union in its ftead[d]. The ftorming party of feamen from the camp at Point Negro, under Captain Rogers, landed at the town of Fort Royal, of which they foon took poffeffion, being aided by

---

[d] The whole fleet, witneffing this gallant action, inftantly faluted the Britifh colours with three hearty cheers.

the firſt battalion of grenadiers, under Lieutenant Colonel Stewart, and third light infantry, under Lieutenant Colonel Cloſe, from Prince Edward's camp at La Coſte.—While this was doing, Lieutenant Colonel Coote kept up a heavy fire of muſketry on the bridge and road, over which the enemy were retreating to throw themſelves into Fort Bourbon; and Captain de Revigne covering the attack of the infantry by a well-directed fire of ſome field pieces, the whole action was ſo eminently ſucceſsful in every part, that it is hard to ſay where was the greateſt glory, every one performing the ſervice allotted to him in ſo excellent a manner. General Rochambeau, ſeeing that all reſiſtance would now be uſeleſs, Fort Royal, his grand depôt of proviſions and ammunition, being loſt, ſent a flag to General Grey, offering terms of capitulation; and commiſſioners being named, who met at the houſe of Madame Dillon to arrange the preliminary articles of it, the terms were finally adjuſted and agreed to on the 22d inſtant; and the ratification thereof being ſigned by the Commanders in Chief on both ſides, on the 23d following, at four o'clock in the afternoon, his Royal Highneſs Major General Prince Edward took poſſeſſion of both gates of the fort with the firſt and third battalions of grenadiers, and firſt and third light infantry. On Tueſday the 25th of March, 1794, the garriſon marched out of Fort Bourbon, to the number of nine hundred men; and being allowed the honours of war for their gallant *de-

---

* The gallant defence made by General Rochambeau and his garriſon was ſtrongly manifeſted on our entering Fort Bourbon, as there was ſcarce an inch of ground untouched by our ſhot or ſhells; and it is but

fence, they marched down the hill with their colours flying; and laying down their arms on the parade of Fort Royal, were embarked on board of fhips which took them immediately to France. Our troops, both army and that part of the navy that had ferved (during the fiege) on fhore, lined the road as the enemy paffed; and entering the fort, they ftruck the French and hoifted the Britifh colours, changing the name from Fort Bourbon to Fort George, in compliment to our gracious Sovereign, which it now bears, and Fort Louis bears the name of Fort Edward.—At the commencement of the fiege the garrifon of Fort Bourbon confifted of one thoufand two hundred men, which were reduced to nine hundred at the conclufion of it. Five ftands of colours laid down by the garrifon, and two colours of Fort Bourbon, were brought to England by Major Grey, fecond fon of his Excellency the Commander in Chief, and prefented by him (with the difpatches) to his Majefty, who ordered them to be hung up in the Cathedral of St. Paul, as a lafting memorial of the gallant action atchieved by Sir Charles Grey and Sir John Jervis, and their brave forces[f]; by

juftice to fay, it did them the higheft honour.—Among the cafualties that happened during the fiege, the following deferves notice. A party of the befieged were in one of the chambers of the Bomb-proof in the Traverfe, when a fhell from one of our batteries fell into the arched way, and rebounding, burft the door of the chamber, and killed the whole party.

[f] It is much to the credit of the officers, who ferved on fhore from the landing on the ifland till the reduction of Fort Bourbon, a period of forty-feven days, that they fhared the fame hardfhips as the privates without a murmur, fleeping in their clothes the whole time; and being fo fituated that they feldom could have the benefit of tents or any kind of hovel, they were expofed continually to the heavy rains and nocturnal damps which in a tropical climate fo feverely try the conftitution; but, owing (as it was imagined) to the flannel fhirts which were invariably worn by all ranks, they, as yet, fuffered lefs from ficknefs than could have been expected.

which one of the moſt valuable of the French iſlands in the Weſt Indies was added to the Britiſh dominions, poſſeſſing (beſides great revenues and prodigious ſources of wealth) one of the fineſt harbours in the world, in which the whole Britiſh fleet might ſafely anchor.

ARTICLES OF CAPITULATION OF FORT BOURBON.

On the 21ſt of March, 1794, by order of their Excellencies Sir Charles Grey, K. B. General and Commander in Chief of his Britannic Majeſty's forces in the Weſt Indies, &c. &c. &c. and Vice Admiral Sir John Jervis, K. B. commanding his Majeſty's fleet, &c. &c. Commodore C. Thompſon, Colonel R. Symes, and Captain J. Conyngham, met at Dillon's houſe to receive propoſals of capitulation for Fort Bourbon, from Colonel d'Aucourt, Captain Dupriret, and Gaſchet Dumaine, jun. nominated Commiſſioners for that purpoſe by General Rochambeau.

The following ARTICLES *were propoſed, diſcuſſed, and modified, at a second conference held at Fort Royal on the 22d of March, 1794.*

Article I. THE garriſon, compoſed of the troops of the line, artillery, gunners of the marine, and national guard, ſhall march out with colours flying, thirty rounds a man, and two field pieces with twelve rounds.—ANSWER. The colony of Martinique, already reduced by the arms of his Britannic Majeſty, and the forts and towns of St. Pierre and Fort Royal taken with ſword in hand, General Rochambeau can only capitulate for Fort Bourbon, and what it contains.—Granted. But they are to lay down their arms at a place ap-

PLAN OF
FORT BOURBON now FORT GEORGE,
in the Island of Martinique.

Explanation.

A Bastion Choiseul.
B Redlt. Redoubt.
1 Arched Cistern
2 Cistern not Arch'd.
3 Officers Barracks.
4 Barracks.
5 Bomb Proof View made in the Traverse.
6 Powder magazine in D.º
7 The Traverse.
8 Officers houses, Armoury.
9 Salve-houses &c.
10 Artillery Store house & magazine.
11 Grand powder magazine.
12 Enpoint Cistern.
13 Fort Royal Gate.

Engraved from an Account of the Expedition
against the French West India Islands,
by the Rev.ª Cooper Willyams, A.M.

Road to Fort Royal

Gallery to the Mine

Scale of Toises.

Longitude 61.12' from London

Published July 1.ˢᵗ 1796, by the Rev.ᵈ Cooper Willyams.

Engraved by S.J. Neele 352 Strand London.

pointed, and not to ferve againſt his Britannic Majeſty, or his allies, during the preſent war.

II. Three months pay to be allowed to the troops of the line.—ANSWER. No pay will be given. All their effects will be allowed them; and they will be provided with whatever may be neceſſary for their voyage to France.

III. The thirty-feventh regiment, formerly Marſhal Turenne's, ſhall keep their colours and arms.—ANSWER. Refuſed, being contrary to all cuſtoms of war. The officers may keep their fwords.

IV. They ſhall be furniſhed with ſhips to carry them to France.—ANSWER. Granted.

V. The emigrants, who have returned to Martinique, ſhall not be preſent where the garriſon lay down their arms or embark.—ANSWER. Granted.

VI. Such perſons of the national guard, who can give proofs of their property, ſhall be permitted to remain in the iſland, giving that property as ſecurity for their conduct.—ANSWER. Thoſe of the national guard in Fort Bourbon who have affairs to fettle, and whoſe fojourn may not be deemed dangerous to the colony, may remain according to the declaration of the General, dated January 1, 1794.

Such as wiſh to go to France ſhall be allowed, leaving their agents here. —ANSWER. Granted.

VII. Perſons not included in the above article, who are compelled to return to France, ſhall be allowed a certain time to fettle their affairs.—ANSWER. A proper time ſhall be allowed: fifteen days at leaſt.

VIII. Perſons belonging to the garriſon of Fort Convention, poſſeſſing no landed property, but who exerciſed ſome profeſſion or trade previous to the preſent capitulation, ſhall be allowed to continue their trade or calling; nor fent to France, provided their future conduct ſhould not make ſuch a meaſure neceſſary.—ANSWER. They are regarded in the ſame predicament with thoſe in Article VI.

IX. The legal regulations of the conſtituted authorities ſhall be confirmed. —ANSWER. Refuſed.

X. The code of civil judicature in force through the ifland fhall be continued for the fpace of two years.—Answer. Granted, till his Britannic Majefty's pleafure be known.

XI. The property of owners and captains of fhips fhall be fecured to them on board and on fhore.—Answer. Granted, as to their property in Fort Bourbon.

XII. The inhabitants of St. Pierre, embarked on Englifh fhips, fhall be fet at liberty, and their property, under feal, fecured to them.—Answer. This article cannot come within the prefent capitulation. The claimants may apply to the commanders of the fleet and army.

XIII. The ordonateur and officers of adminiftration fhall have permiffion and time to regulate their accounts, and to take with them the papers relative to that end.—Answer. Granted.

XIV. There fhall be an entire and abfolute oblivion of the paft, and an end to all animofities.—Answer. Granted, according to the proclamations.

XV. The rights of free citizens inrolled in the national guard fhall be preferved.—Answer. Refufed.

XVI. The liberty of individuals compofing the companies of l'Enclume, d'Octavius, de la Croire, and de Pontouur, fhall be confirmed.—Answer. Refufed. The flaves muft be reftored to their owners.

XVII. A period fhall be fixed for the taking poffeffion of the fort, and the neceffary time allowed for the garrifon to take out their effects.—Answer. The two gates of Fort Bourbon to be delivered up to the troops of his Britannic Majefty immediately after the exchange of the prefent articles. The garrifon will march out at the great gate, and be conducted to the place appointed for each corps, by the commiffioners who have managed the prefent capitulation, and will lay down their arms at the place of their embarkation. Three days will be allowed for the evacuation of the fort, and the commiffaries of artillery and ftores will remain in the forts to take inventories of all the magazines.

XVIII. The greateſt attention ſhall be paid to the ſick and wounded; and they ſhall be furniſhed with ſhips to carry them to France as they recover. —ANSWER. Granted; but at the expence of the French government, and to be attended by their own ſurgeons; if not ſufficient for the purpoſe, ſurgeons ſhall be furniſhed.

XIX. General Rochambeau, immediately upon the ſurrender of the fort, ſhall be at liberty to take his meaſures for his return to France. A frigate to be furniſhed him, his aides de camp, ſecretaries, and ſuite.—ANSWER. A commodious veſſel ſhall be allowed to General Rochambeau, with the neceſſary paſſports for his ſafe return to France.

XX. The effects, trunks, cheſts, private papers, and all that General Rochambeau ſhall declare to belong to himſelf and ſuite, ſhall be put under the protection of an Engliſh guard, when the troops of that nation ſhall have taken poſſeſſion of Fort Convention, and ſhall be embarked with him.— ANSWER. Granted.

XXI. The civil ordonateur, or intendant of the colony, ſhall have liberty alſo, with the officers of adminiſtration, comptroller and treaſurer, with thoſe employed in the public offices at St. Pierre and Fort Royal, to return to France.—ANSWER. Granted.

XXII. The ſame demands made by General Rochambeau in Art. XX. ſhall be granted to the intendant and thoſe under him.—ANSWER. Granted.

XXIII. All papers of accounts in the forts or town ſhall be carefully collected by the principals of each department to which they belong, and embarked in the ſame ſhip with the ordonateur.—ANSWER. All papers, not eſſential to be left in the colony, ſhall be given, and free acceſs to take authentic copies of ſuch as it may be thought neceſſary to retain.

XXIV. Captains and officers of merchant ſhips, who have not ſettled their affairs, ſhall be allowed time to do ſo. The former the ſpace of four months, the latter of two months, under the protection of the commander of his Britannic Majeſty's forces, that they may recover their debts; after which they will

L

procure the readiest paffage to whatever place may be expedient for their affairs, with paffports from the Englifh commanders.—Answer. Granted.

Additional Article. Fort Bourbon to be delivered up to his Britannic Majefty in its prefent ftate, with no deterioration of its batteries, mines, magazines of artillery or provifions, and every thing it contains which is not the private property of the garrifon.

Fort Royal, March 22, 1794.

Signed.

D'Aucourt.	C. Thompson.
Gaschet, Fils.	Rich. Symes.
Dupriret.	John Conyngham.

Approved by me,	Approved by us,
Dte. Rochambeau,	Charles Grey.
Commander in Chief of the French	John Jervis.
Weft India Iflands.	

On the 21ft of March Captain Faulknor was promoted from the Zebra floop to the command of the Bienvenue French frigate of 40 guns, taken in the Carénage of Fort Royal, and which was now named the Undaunted by the Admiral, to exprefs the greatnefs of that action, which finifhed the capture of the whole ifland. At the fame time Lieutenant Bowen was promoted to the command of the Zebra floop, for his gallant conduct on the 17th inftant, as well as at various other times.

The gun-boats, which by the French were called "Les Petit Diables," were of infinite fervice, and gained the officers commanding them immortal credit, by the fteady and well-directed fire they kept up conftantly, both night and day, on Fort Louis; and though continually expofed to an heavy fire both of grape and round fhot, their lofs was fmall, not more than four killed and wounded, during the fiege. The feveral fhips of the line contributed their aid, by fending row-boats armed to attend them in cafe of accident.

CHAPTER VIII.

GENERAL PRESCOTT IS LEFT GOVERNOR OF MARTINIQUE . . . .
THE COMMANDERS IN CHIEF SAIL FOR ST. LUCIA . . . . GENE-
RAL DUNDAS LANDS NEAR PIGEON ISLAND . . . . THE FLEET
ANCHORS AT MARIGOT DE ROSSEAUX . . . . PRINCE EDWARD
LANDS WITH THE GRENADIERS, AND MARCHES TOWARDS
MORNE FORTUNE' . . . . COLONEL COOTE LANDS WITH THE
LIGHT INFANTRY . . . . THE FLEET ANCHORS IN BARRING-
TON'S BAY . . . . COLONEL COOTE STORMS A REDOUBT ON THE
MORNE . . . . GENERAL RICARD SURRENDERS THE ISLAND . . . .
COLONEL SIR CHARLES GORDON LEFT GOVERNOR OF ST. LUCIA
. . . . THE COMMANDERS IN CHIEF SAIL TO MARTINIQUE.

His Excellency the Commander in Chief, having left Lieutenant
General Prefcott to command at Martinique, with the fifteenth,
thirty-ninth, fifty-eighth, fixty-fourth, and feventieth regiments
to garrifon that ifland, on the 30th of March he embarked the
following troops on board his Majefty's fhips in the bay of Fort
Royal, viz. the brigade of grenadiers, commanded by his Royal
Highnefs Prince Edward; the brigade of light infantry, under
command of Major General Dundas; and the fixth, ninth, and

forty-third regiments, commanded by Colonel Sir Charles Gordon; with engineers under Colonel Dornford, and a detachment of Royal artillery, with some light ordnance, under Lieutenant Colonel Paterson.—On the 31st the Admiral made the signal for the fleet to sail by eleven A. M. and by half past nine the next morning was off the north part of the island of St. Lucia, where he lay to for the rest of the fleet that had fallen to leeward. Every thing having been previously arranged between the General and Admiral, they effected three different landings on the island with little resistance, and no loss. By half past one P. M. Major General Dundas's division, consisting of the third battalion of light infantry, under Lieutenant Colonel Close, and conducted by Captains Kelly and Lord Garlies of the navy, made good their landing at Ance du Cap, not far from Le Gros Islet[g]; and the second light infantry, under Lieutenant Colonel Blundell, conducted by Commodore Thompson, at Ance du Chocque, who were ordered to join the first column, taking the enemy's batteries in reverse, and to occupy a position for the purpose of investing the works of Morne Fortuné on the side of the Carénage; all which, notwithstanding a sharp fire kept up by the enemy from several small batteries, was executed by General Dundas with his usual spirit and abilities. As the Boyne and the rest of the fleet passed along the coast they received the fire of many small forts and batteries, without returning it; and though considerably within the range of their shot, which passed over and through their sails and

---

[g] By us called Pigeon Island. On it is a very strong battery, which commands a great distance.

rigging, not a man was hurt in any of them. At four P. M. the fleet anchored in twenty fathom water, within a cable's length of the fhore, at Marigot de Rofeaux; at which place his Royal High-nefs Prince Edward with the grenadiers landed about fix o'clock in the evening, under the immediate direction of the Admiral, and began their march foon after. At night they halted on the heights oppofite to Morne Fortuné, from which they were fepa-rated by the Grand Cul de Sac, or Barrington's Bay. Soon after fun-fet, Lieutenant Colonel Coote, with the firft battalion of light infantry, landed from the Boyne at Ance de la Tocque, proceeded to and took the four-gun battery of Ciceron, invefting Morne Fortuné on that fide; at the fame time covering Cul de Sac, or Barrington's Bay, for the entrance of our fleet, which anchored there the next morning, being the 2d of April. This morning early the Prince difpatched two companies of grenadiers, with Lieutenant Smyth of the 7th regiment, his brigade major, to attack two batteries on the coaft, which they found evacuated, with the tri-coloured flag ftill flying; this they brought off with them, and fpiked the guns. Sir Charles Grey, vifiting the Prince's quarters, found his men were halted in a very fwampy and unhealthy place, and ordered them to change their ground, and move on to a houfe at the bottom of Morne Fortuné, which they performed that night without any lofs, though part of their road (near a mile in length) was expofed to the fire of the fort on the Morne, as alfo of a little two-gun battery on a point of land under the fort, which, as they paffed the ravine at the head of the Grand Cul de Sac, played upon them with round fhot and grape: however, the diftance was too great for any mifchief to happen from the latter. In their march they had to pafs a fwampy thicket of plantain trees, which concealed them from the view of the enemy, who neverthelefs kept up a conftant fire of random fhot; and though the diftance was now very trifling, and the cannonade extremely heavy for a long time, not a man was killed, and a few only flightly hurt by the fplinters of ftones and rock which flew in great plenty round them.——Early in the morning of the 3d of April, Lieutenant Colonel Coote, with four light companies, ftormed a redoubt and two batteries clofe to the enemy's principal work on the Morne, and killed two officers and thirty men, made one prifoner (a furgeon), and liberated one Britifh feaman from captivity: he then fpiked fix pieces of cannon, and fell back to Morne Ferré, where he eftablifhed his quarters[h]. The Commander in Chief now determined to carry the works on Morne Fortuné by affault, and accordingly a plan was formed for a general attack to be made on it the next morning by the troops which now invefted it, aided by a party of feamen under command of Lord Garlies: but General Ricard, perceiving the determined behaviour of our troops, prevented the plan being put in execution, by agreeing to terms of capitulation, which had been offered by Sir Charles Grey, who

[h] The conduct and abilities of Colonel Coote in this enterprife gained him the particular thanks of the Commander in Chief, whofe orders he had fo ably executed; and he was well fupported by the whole of his department, particularly by Major Evatt, Captains Buchanan, Crofbie, Welch, Thomas Grey (one of the General's aid de camps), and Stovin; alfo by Major of Brigade Vifcher, with Lieutenant Drozier, and the detachment of royal artillery, who fpiked the guns.

had fent in Major Maitland with a flag of truce to fummon the garrifon to furrender. The gates of the fort were put into our poffeffion the fame evening by nine o'clock. On the 4th the enemy marched out of the fort, with the honours of war, to the glacis, where they piled their arms, and were embarked on board of tranfports, which conveyed them to France, under conditions that they fhould not ferve againft his Britannic Majefty during the war[i]. When his Royal Highnefs Prince Edward marched into the fort of Morne Fortuné, and hoifted the Britifh colours, he changed its name to Fort Charlotte, in honour of his auguft parent.—Major Maitland had been difpatched to Pigeon Ifland with a fummons, which, by order of General Ricard, was delivered up to his Majefty's troops on the fame terms as the Morne. The Commander in Chief left the fixth and ninth regiments, with detachments of artillery and engineers, as a garrifon for this ifland, under the command of Colonel Sir Charles Gordon, who was appointed governor till his Majefty's pleafure was known.

The ifland of St. Lucia had its name from the day, dedicated to the virgin martyr St. Lucia, on which it was difcovered. It is about fix leagues fouth of Martinique, and twenty-one north-weft from Barbadoes: it is fifteen miles long, and eleven broad; is very hilly, and covered in a great many places with thick woods, of

---

[i] The garrifon that marched out with General Ricard, and laid down their arms as prifoners of war, were about three hundred men, troops of the line (among which one hundred and twenty-five were of the regiment d'Aunai), fome artillery, and a few people of colour. General Ricard, at his own requeft, was fent to America, as had been General Rochambeau, who chofe that place in preference to his own diftracted country, where the fyftem of blood that was then the order of the day under the tyranny of Robefpierre, would have immolated even thefe men, who had with fo much bravery defended the pofts intrufted to them by their country.

whofe timber the planters of Martinique and the neighbouring iflands build their houfes and mills The fuftic and cocoa tree is found here alfo in great abundance. This ifland has frequently changed its mafters, being alternately poffeffed by the French and Englifh: it has many good bays and harbours, and is well watered by feveral fine clear rivers. Two of the mountains are faid to have been volcanos. Morne Fortuné is a high hill which overhangs Baffe Terre, the principal town of the ifland. On the fummit of the Morne is a fortification, as yet unfinifhed; by nature it is very ftrong, but art has done little for it; for, when the outworks fall, the fort is incapable of withftanding a fiege. We found but little ammunition or military ftores, and one fmall uncovered tank was the only refervoir for water. Here is alfo a Pigeon Ifland, which is called by the French Gros Iflet, and is fo ftrongly fortified both by nature and art, that if it was well fupplied with provifions and ftores, would be capable of braving a very formidable attack. The bay of the Grand Cul de Sac is a fine harbour for fhips of any fize to ride in, during the hurricane months.

Lieutenant D'Arcy Prefton, being promoted from a lieutenancy in the Boyne to the command of the Rattlefnake floop of war, failed for England this day, carrying Captain Mafon, one of the aid de camps of the Commander in Chief, and Captain Parker of the Blanche, with an account of the further fuccefs of his Majefty's arms in the reduction of the ifland of St. Lucia[k], happily effected without the lofs of a fingle man, though there had been a

---

[k] The General tranfmitted alfo a plan of the projected works on Morne-Fortuné, earneftly recommending them to be finifhed, as it was a very ftrong poft, not commanded, but commanding every other poft around it.

good deal of cannonading from the enemy's batteries and works. The flank battalions being reimbarked on board of their refpective fhips, and Sir Charles Grey with his fuite being as ufual with the Admiral on board the Boyne, the whole fleet weighed and made fail from this ifland by eight in the morning of the 5th of April, and by nine at night they anchored in Fort Royal harbour, Martinique. Thus, in the fhort period of fomething more than two months, by the efforts of this army and navy, inconfiderable indeed in numbers, but united in an ardent defire to prove themfelves faithful to their country, and ftrenuous to defend and promote her welfare, and increafe her confequence, was the Britifh ftandard a fecond time hoifted on the walls of a republican fortrefs, and another ifland added to the Britifh dominions.

To provide for the future order and good government of their conquefts was now the tafk of Sir Charles Grey and his friend and colleague, Sir John Jervis; and as, in the attainment of them, their hearts and counfels were in unifon, fo in this moft arduous bufinefs were their united exertions employed to eftablifh a fyftem of government for the conquered iflands, which might be equally ferviceable to their country, as conciliatory to the minds of the newly acquired fubjects of it; but at a moment like this, when they were pufhing on from one field of conflict and glory to another, it was impoffible to render any fyftem of government perfect; they therefore thought that the beft mode would be to leave them a government which appeared to have been moft defired by the majority of the people, and which agreed better with our own forms than the wild confufion of democratic and revolutionary power. Accordingly, they for the prefent left them in the exercife of their accuftomed laws, fuch as they had been at the happieft period of their own government, and which appeared beft calculated to forward a fyftem of confidence among their own order, and to prepare them for that form of government (we from experience know the bleffings of, and) which unqueftionably, on the fame experience, would become earneftly defired by all ranks of people. To further alfo the defirable object of conciliating the minds of the conquered by an act of moderation and indulgence, the conduct of all civil affairs[1] was principally entrufted to thofe whofe influence in the colony pointed them out as proper to be confided in; and whilft every tendency to licentioufnefs would be checked by the vigorous direction of General Prefcott under his military government, the former courts, for the adminiftration of juftice agreeable to the laws and cuftoms before the revolution, were allowed to go on, that the affections and gratitude of his majefty's new fubjects might in the fureft manner be attached and fecured. However an arrangement of officers, guided by the conftitution of the other Britifh colonies, was not neglected, and accordingly feveral nominations were made and tranfmitted home for approval. St. Lucia was left in the fame ftate, as to its government, as Martinique.

---

[1] The revenue department was however an exception to this arrangement of the civil departments, as the the purpofe of trade could not of courfe be anfwered through the forms of a French cuftom-houfe, or the revenue laws adhered to but by the eftablifhment of our own people to carry on that neceffary branch. Thofe places therefore in the diftrict of the ifland of Martinique, which were immediately neceffary to be filled, were attended to, and a lift of them fent home, that when his majefty's pleafure fhould be made known with regard to the future civil government, they might be put in motion without any delay.

CHAPTER IX.

EXPEDITION AGAINST GUADALOUPE .... THE ISLES DE SAINTS
ATTACKED AND TAKEN .... THE BOYNE AND VETERAN AN-
CHOR OFF GROZIER .... THE TROOPS LAND UNDER COVER OF
THE WINCHELSEA FRIGATE .... CAPTAIN LORD GARLIES
WOUNDED .... FORT FLEUR D'EPEE TAKEN BY STORM ....
FORT LOUIS AND THE TOWN OF POINT A PITRE TAKEN ....
CASUALTIES .... GENERAL DESCRIPTION OF THE ISLAND.

ON Tuesday the 8th of April, the fleet[m], having the Commander
in Chief on board, with the remainder of the forces which were
not left to garrison the two islands of Martinique and St. Lucia,
weighed anchor by seven o'clock A.M. and sailed from the bay
of Fort Royal on an expedition against Guadaloupe (the troops
having been previously shifted from the men of war to the transports). The Admiral detached Captain Rogers in the Quebec
frigate, Captain Faulknor in the Blanche, Captain Incledon in the
Ceres, and Captain Scott in the Rose, to attack a cluster of small
islands called the Saints, lying between Dominique and Guada-

[m] Consisting of the Boyne, Irresistible, Veteran, Winchelsea, Solebay, Quebec, Ceres, Blanche, Rose,
Woolwich, Experiment, and Roebuck, together with the transports with troops, and the ordnance and hospital ships and victuallers.

loupe, which they executed with much fpirit and gallantry: having landed a party of their feamen and marines, they carried them without any lofs on their part, on the morning of the 10th inftant; and when the fleet arrived the fame morning off the iflands, they had the fatisfaction of perceiving the union flag hoifted on their two commanding batteries. Thefe iflands are valued principally on account of a fmall harbour, where a few fhips of war may ride in fafety during the hurricane months; and alfo that they overlook a good deal of the coaft of Baffe Terre.—About noon on the 10th of April the Boyne and Veteran anchored in the bay of Point à Pitre, off the village of Grozier, and fome more of the fleet in the courfe of the afternoon; but a frefh wind and lee current prevented moft of the tranfports from getting in till the day after. Without waiting however for the arrival of all the troops, the General determined to land thofe that were with him, immediately; and accordingly the firft and fecond battalions of grenadiers, one company of the forty-third regiment, fifty marines, and four hundred feamen detached by the Admiral, under the command of Captain George Grey of the Boyne, made good their landing by one o'clock in the morning of the 11th, under a fevere fire from Fort Fleur d'Epée, and a three-gun battery at Grozier. As it was impoffible for them to land without the latter being filenced, Lord Garlies in the Winchelfea was ordered on that fervice, which he performed in a mafterly manner, laying his fhip within half-mufket fhot of the battery, as near indeed as the depth of water would allow him to approach; and after a ſmart fire for ſome time on both ſides, he drove them from their guns, and the troops then effected their landing without any loſs. In this buſineſs, though every ſhot from the battery hit ſome part of the Winchelſea, cutting the maſts and rigging, Lord Garlies was the only man wounded, receiving a bad contuſion in his face. Some more of the troops having arrived on the 11th, the General, perceiving the enemy to be in conſiderable force at the ſtrong poſt of Fort Fleur d'Epée, determined to attack them without loſs of time, and accordingly arranged his plans in the following order: the firſt diviſion, under command of his Royal Highneſs Prince Edward, conſiſting of the firſt and ſecond battalions of grenadiers and one hundred of the naval battalion, was to attack the poſt on Morne Maſcot, an height within muſket-ſhot of the fort; the ſecond diviſion, commanded by Major General Dundas, conſiſting of the firſt and ſecond battalions of light infantry, and one hundred of the naval battalion, to attack the fort of Fleur d'Epée in the rear, and to cut off its communication with Fort Louis and Point à Pitre; and the third diviſion, commanded by Colonel Symes, conſiſting of the third battalion of grenadiers and the third battalion of light infantry, and the remainder of the naval battalions, to proceed by the road on the ſea-ſide to co-operate with Major General Dundas. The ſoldiers were particularly directed not to fire, but truſt ſolely to the bayonet; and the ſeamen, who were commanded by Captain Nugent and Captain Faulknor, to uſe their pikes and ſwords; all which was moſt ſcrupulouſly obeyed; the ſeveral diviſions having marched earlier, ac-

cording to the diftance they had to go, that they might commence
the attack at the fame inftant. The fignal for the attack, which
was a gun from the Boyne, was given by the Admiral at five
o'clock in the morning of the 12th. The troops moved forward
with the moft determined intrepidity. As they advanced to the
firft picquet the alarm was given; the out-pofts were driven in,
or put to death; and in an inftant the fides of the hill on which
the fort was fituated were covered by our people, who fcrambled
up, under a moft tremendous difcharge of grape fhot and mufketry: fome failors jumped into the embrafures, driving the enemy before: the foldiers, who had reached the gates, at length
fucceeded in forcing them open, and a fcene of dreadful conflict
took place: the enemy ftill continuing to make a ftout refiftance,
were put to the fword in great numbers; at length, as many as
could efcape through the gates and embrafures, or by leaping over
the walls, fled with the utmoft precipitation towards the town of
Point à Pitre. Our victorious troops foon followed, driving them
acrofs the Carénage to Baffe Terre, whither they and feveral of
the inhabitants made their efcape in boats, before the Ceres and
two gun-boats could get into the Carénage to cut off their retreat,
though this fervice was performed by Captain Incledon with the
greateft alertnefs. With Fleur d'Epée fell Hog Ifland, and Fort
Louis, an old fortification commanding the entrance into the harbour of Point à Pitre, which town alfo was taken poffeffion of at
the fame time by Sir Charles Grey. Our lofs in this action was
confiderable, in proportion to the fmallnefs of our numbers, being

fifty-four killed and wounded; the enemy loft in all two hundred and fifty. Fort Fleur d'Epée is ftrongly fituated on the fummit of a hill, two fides of which are towards the fea, from whence it has a very formidable appearance; but being commanded by Morne Mafcot, when that falls into the power of an enemy it is of little confequence. On the brow of the hill, a little below the fort, is an half-moon battery, which commands a great diftance along the coaft. Among the many accidents worth notice, I beg leave to mention the following, which I hope will be a ftriking inftance (among many of the fame kind which have happened this war) that it behoves all our people ferving on fhore, whether military or naval, to be diftinguifhed by red dreffes. The French, as well as feveral other continental troops, are dreffed in blue; of courfe, in the confufion of an affault, efpecially if it happens before day-break, a feaman's blue jacket may, and I am convinced often has, been the caufe of his death by the hands of his own countrymen. A feaman of the Boyne, belonging to the firft company, expreffing a wifh that he might have an opportunity of lowering the French flag, and hoifting our own; and being a remarkably fine fellow, was pitched upon to carry the union flag on this attack for that purpofe, in cafe the fort fhould be taken; and accordingly it was wrapped in many folds round him, and he was to defend it as well as he could. When he approached the fort, the firft object that attracted his notice was the flag-ftaff, and, regardlefs of every danger, he rufhed forward, pike in hand; and having once got into the fort, away he ran to the defired fpot, and had

N

already ftruck the tri-coloured flag, and was endeavouring to dif-
engage himfelf from his wrapper, in order to hoift that in its
ftead, when fome foldiers coming fuddenly round the corner of a
building, and taking him for one of the enemy, in an inftant attacked him, and he fell feverely wounded before they difcovered
their miftake. I am happy however to add, that the poor fellow, by the care and fkill of Mr. Weir, the furgeon-general° of
the navy, recovered fufficiently to fhew, before the end of the
campaign, that his courage was undiminifhed by the accident.——
Captain Faulknor, who had fo eminently diftinguifhed himfelf at
the capture of Fort Louis in Martinique, had a narrow efcape in
this bufinefs: having led his men on to the affault with his ufual
gallantry, he was encountered by a French officer, whom he inftantly ftruck at with his fword, which falling on the epaulette on
his fhoulder, did not penetrate: the Frenchman clofed with him,
and being the ftrongeft man, threw him to the ground; and, wreft-
ing the fword from his hand, was in the act of plunging it into
his body, when fortunately a feaman belonging to the Boyne, feeing the danger his gallant leader was in, with his pike pinned his
adverfary to the earth.——As at this time I was the only chaplain

° As this is an office, I believe, hitherto unknown in the navy, I fhall explain the reafon of its being now
eftablifhed. The Admiral had in a former war experienced the attention and zeal of Mr. Weir, and being
well acquainted with the fatigue and danger that would unavoidably be the lot of his furgeon, if he did his
duty, he pitched upon him for that office, and as an encouragement he procured permiffion to appoint a furgeon general to the navy, and his appointment did honour to his difcernment. Mr. Weir was indefatigable
in attending the wounded and fick in his own fhip, and equally ready to vifit others; and even where his duty
had no demand on him, his humanity led him to give his advice and affiftance. In his mode of treatment of
that dreadful difeafe, the yellow fever, he was more fuccefsful than was generally the cafe, as the Boyne loft a
lefs proportion of patients under that afflicting malady than any other fhip on the expedition.

on the expedition (Mr. Ruxton, chaplain of the fifty-fixth regiment, having died foon after his landing in Martinique), and feveral of our men having fallen in this gallant attack, I went on fhore up to Fort Fleur d'Epée to pay the laft honours to our unfortunate countrymen, eighteen of whom were killed on the fpot. The fcene I beheld furpaffed my powers of defcription. It was early in the morning, foon after the action was over. At the foot of the hill lay feveral of our feamen badly wounded, waiting to be carried on board their refpective fhips: a little further, under the tall trees that grew within a few yards of the fea, feveral naval officers repofing after the fatigues of the morning, and their men not far from them. As we went up the hill we met fome of the wounded prifoners brought in by our people; and at the gates of the fort was an heap of the flain, who had all died by the fword or bayonet. Within the fort the deftruction appeared more dreadful, being more confined; a multitude of miferable wretches expiring of their wounds, and many of our own people in the fame fituation: in the midft of this was his Excellency writing his difpatches on a table, on which, fatigued with the action, an artilleryman was fleeping, whom the General would by no means have difturbed; one proof among thoufands that the trueft heroifm may be, and often is, united to the greateft humanity.—It would be invidious to mention particularly, who diftinguifhed themfelves in this bufinefs, where all feemed emulous of glory; but as the greateft refponfibility is attached to the higher ranks, it will be but juftice to fay, that Prince Edward, General Dundas,

Colonels Symes, Cradock, and Coote, with the other officers of rank, as alfo Captains Nugent and Faulknor, the officers commanding the naval battalions, received the thanks of the Commander in Chief in public orders, for their excellent conduct and refolution, difplayed through the whole of the action.

Point à Pitre is the capital of that part of Guadaloupe called Grand Terre, which is feparated from the other part, called Bafs Terre, by a narrow arm of the fea, in form of a river; it is called the river Sallée. The town is neat and well built, but in an unhealthy fituation, being on the borders of a large extent of fwampy land; it has a good harbour called the Carénage, the entrance to which is guarded on one fide by an half-moon battery lately erected on Iflet a Couchon, or Hog Ifland, and on the other by the ancient caftle of Fort Louis; it is alfo defended on the land fide by a hill called Morne Government, on which is a ftrong battery. The country on this part of Guadaloupe is remarkably flat, forming a ftrong contraft to Baffe Terre, which gradually rifes from the feafhore till it forms a chain of hills extending from one end of that part of the ifland to the other.

CHAPTER X.

THE GENERAL EMBARKS HIS ARMY, AND LANDS ON BASSE TERRE
AT PETIT BOURG .... OCCURRENCES ON THE MARCH TOWARDS
PALMISTE .... THE ADMIRAL ANCHORS IN ANCE DE BAILLIF
.... GENERAL DUNDAS LANDS, AND FORMS A COMMUNICA-
TION WITH SIR CHARLES GREY .... THE PALMISTE TAKEN
BY ASSAULT ... GENERAL COLLOT DELIVERS UP FORT SAINT
CHARLES AND THE ISLAND OF GUADALOUPE AND ITS DE-
PENDENCIES TO THE COMMANDERS IN CHIEF.

On the 13th, the forty-third regiment being landed to garrifon
Fort Prince of Wales (late Fleur d'Epée), the town of Point à Pitre, and the other pofts on Grand Terre, the General and the reft
of his army reimbarked on board of their refpective fhips; and in
the evening the Sea Flower brig, Captain Pierrepoint, failed for
England with difpatches. At twelve o'clock the next day, the
Quebec and the other frigates, with the tranfports, failed over to
the other fide of the bay; and in the afternoon the troops, confifting of the grenadiers and light infantry, commanded by his
Royal Highnefs Prince Edward, landed at a village called Petit
Bourg, where many of the principal people of the ifland were af-

fembled, who received the Commander in Chief and the Prince with the greateft demonftrations of joy. A party of failors alfo, under the command of Captain Rogers of the Quebec, landed at the fame time. That night the General returned to the Boyne; the next morning he landed at St. Mary's, where he found Colonel Coote, with the firft battalion of light infantry, who had marched in before day-break from Petit Bourg. The troops now marched forward, principally along fhore, without any remarkable occurrence, and halted for the night at a fmall village between Cabes Terre and Petit Bourg. On the 16th the troops, ftill advancing along fhore, reached Trou Chien, a very ftrong poft, which the enemy had abandoned; and before dark the army halted on the high ground over Les Trois Riverres, from whence they faw the enemy's two redoubts and their ftrong pofts on the heights of Palmifte. The General intended to have attacked the enemy that night; but the troops were too much fatigued from the long and difficult march they had juft finifhed. Here, at a beautiful plantation belonging to Monfieur Bellifle, the Prince and feveral of his officers were fumptuoufly entertained at fupper by that gentleman, who repeated his hofpitality the next day. All this time the Admiral ftood off and on near the fhore, to be ready to pour in affiftance in cafe there fhould be any neceffity for it: but on the army retiring up the country towards Palmifte on the 17th inftant, he came round towards the town of Baffe Terre. Fort St. Charles fired a few fhot and fhells at the Boyne without effect. At half paft one P. M. we were becalmed off the town, and had a beautiful view of the country round it, which, rifing gradually inland, prefents a varied amphitheatre of plantations, woods, hills, and vallies, interfperfed with elegant and well-built houfes, orna-mented by many fine plantations of palms, cocoa-nut, and other tall and majeftic trees. By five P. M. we anchored in Ance de Baillif, about a mile from the town of Baffe Terre, which was hid from our view by an high point of land forming the bay. On the 17th Major General Dundas, with the third battalion of grena-diers, and fecond and third battalions of light infantry, landed at Vieux Habitant, fome miles north-weft of Baffe Terre, meeting with little oppofition and no lofs, taking poffeffion of Morne Magdalene, and deftroying two batteries, then detaching Lieu-tenant Colonel Blundell with the fecond battalion of light infan-try, he in the night forced feveral difficult pofts of the enemy. On the 17th General Sir Charles Grey made a difpofition for the attack of a redoubt called d'Arbaud, and a battery named d'Anet, both near Grand Ance; the troops pufhed forward, and halted within a league of the village of Trois Riviere. By day-break on the 18th Lieutenant Colonel Coote, with the firft battalion of light infantry, attacked and ftormed the battery; every man in it was either killed, wounded, or made prifoner, and not one of our own was hurt. At the fame time the grenadiers were ordered to ad-vance againft the redoubt, which was commanded by this battery, and which they found had been deferted by the enemy early in the night, who burnt and deftroyed every thing in and near it. On the night of the 17th inftant, the enemy in the town of Baffe

Terre (being divided in their opinions, and party running very
high among them) fet fire to the town, the whole of the weft
end of which was confumed, containing much valuable property,
and many fine houfes. The motives for this mifchief we never
could learn, as they were at that time in full poffeffion of the
town; and as it was entirely commanded by Fort St. Charles,
there could be no danger of its falling into our hands until the
fort was taken. At one oclock in the morning of the 20th, the
Commander in Chief, at the head of his troops, advanced to the
attack of the principal dependance of the enemy, which was a
chain of batteries on the heights of Palmifte, extending above
a league. The grenadiers were commanded by Prince Edward,
and the light infantry by Lieutenant Colonel Coote. At five in
the morning the attack commenced by the light infantry advancing to the affault of the higheft and moft formidable battery,
which, though well defended by nature and art, was foon obliged
to yield to the fuperior activity and bravery of our troops, who
with their bayonets forced the works, putting thirty of them to
death. It is remarkable, that in this affair the three firft fentries
at the advanced batteries, on firing their mufkets on the alarm,
fhot two advanced men of the light infantry and their guide. The
inftant our men had made themfelves mafters of this poft, perceiving that it commanded all the others, they with infinite fpirit and
addrefs turned the guns againft them, under cover of which our
troops marched up and took them all in fucceffion, without much
further oppofition, although, by every appearance, they had de-

termined to make a vigorous refiftance, having felled trees and laid them acrofs the road, and at the entrance of their batteries, and the guns being moftly loaded with grape-fhot, or bags of mufket balls, it feemed as if they expected to have come to clofe quarters. General Dundas had now formed a communication with Sir Charles Grey by Morne Howell, and the Palmifte (the key of the town and Fort St. Charles) being thus in our poffeffion, the governor, Monfieur Collot, fent a flag of truce to Sir Charles Grey, offering to deliver up Guadaloupe and its dependencies on the fame terms as had been granted to General Rochambeau at Martinique, and Ricard at St. Lucia: the garrifon to march out with the honours of war, and lay down their arms, and to be fent to France, on condition that they fhould not ferve againft the Britifh forces and their allies during the war; General Collot and his fuite to be allowed a certain time to fettle their affairs, and to be conveyed to North America in a frigate. Accordingly, the light infantry being left in the batteries on the Palmifte, the remainder of the troops marched down and took poffeffion of the gates of both town and fort that night. The next day the Boyne weighed anchor, and was towed by boats round from the bay of Baillif to the road of Baffe Terre, where fhe anchored within a cable s length of the fhore. At night a defign of the garrifon, to rife upon our people and murder them, was happily made known to General Dundas, who inftantly rode down to the fort, and took the neceffary precautions to prevent the completion of this infamous plot. At eight o'clock in the morning of Tuefday the 22d of

April the French garrifon of Fort St. Charles marched out, confifting of fifty-five regulars of the regiment of Guadaloupe, and
the fourteenth regiment of France, and eight hundred and eighteen
national guards and others; Prince Edward, with the grenadiers
and light infantry, taking poffeffion immediately, ftruck the republican and hoifted the Britifh colours, changing the name of it
to Fort Matilda. From the returns found among General Collot's
papers it appeared that the number of men capable of bearing
arms in the ifland of Guadaloupe was at that time five thoufand
eight hundred and feventy-feven; and the number of fire-arms
actually delivered out to them was four thoufand and forty-four[p].
On the 26th Prince Edward with his fuite embarked on board the
Blanche frigate, commanded by Captain Faulknor, and failed for
North America; his regiment, the feventh or royal fuzileers, being
ftationed at Quebec. The fpirit and enterprife of his Royal Highnefs on this expedition, with his ftrict attention to difcipline, merits the higheft applaufe, and defervedly gained him the refpect and
efteem of all who ferved with him. Before the troubles (occafioned by the revolution) commenced in thefe iflands, the town of
Baffe Terre was a place of very confiderable traffic, and much re-
forted to by merchants and others: it is regularly built, well wa-

[p] Lieutenant George Vaughan of the Boyne was this day promoted to the command of the Zebra floop,
and the Chaplain of the Boyne was appointed to the chaplaincy of the garrifon of Guadaloupe, there being no
other chaplain on the expedition; but government at home did not think fit to confirm the appointment.
Lieutenant Davers of the Boyne was promoted to be acting commander of the Infpector, from whence he was
promoted to the command of the Bull Dog floop. Lieutenant Ogle was alfo appointed acting commander of
the Affurance.

tered, and beautifully fituated on the fea-fhore, and well defended by feveral batteries and forts, particularly to the eaftward by Fort St. Charles (now called Fort Matilda), which is a regular fortification of great ftrength and extent; but being commanded by furrounding high lands, particularly Houelmont, a fteep hill, on which is a battery that overlooks, not only the fort and town, but the bay, and much of the country near it, it is incapable of maintaining a long defence againft a powerful attack by land, but is impregnable by any that can be made againft it from the fea only. In the centre of the main ftreet is a fpacious walk fhaded by handfome well grown trees, which forms an agreeable relief from the heat which in this climate is fo very oppreffive. Above the town is a large and commodious hofpital, which at this period we found of infinite ufe. The ifland of Guadaloupe was difcovered by Columbus, who named it after fome mountains in Spain to which it bore refemblance, but by the native Caraibs it is called Karukera: it is fituated thirty leagues N. W. from Martinique, and is reckoned the largeft and moft valuable ifland the French held in thefe parts; and, from its vicinity to Antigua and Dominica, as well as to feveral of our fmaller iflands, is of great confequence to us. The ifland is divided into two parts by a narrow channel called La Riviere Sallée, or the Salt River: the eaftern part is called Grand Terre, and is comparatively flat; it is nineteen leagues long and nine broad: the weftern part is properly called Guadaloupe, but is now known by the name of Baffe Terre, and is again fubdivided (by a ridge of mountains extending from

one end to the other) into Capes Terre and Baffe Terre: this part
of the ifland is thirteen leagues and a half in length, and about
feven at the broadeft part.   The iflands immediately dependent
on Guadaloupe are Marigalante, Defeada, and the Saints.   Marigalante is of a round form, about forty miles to the S. E. of Guadaloupe; it is about five leagues long and four broad, and was difcovered by Columbus in 1493, who gave it the name of his own
fhip.   Defeada, or Defirada (that is, the Defirable Ifland), was the
firft of thefe iflands difcovered by Columbus in his fecond voyage
in 1493; it is about fifteen miles N. E. of Guadaloupe, and is not
very fertile.   The Saints are a clufter of iflands on the S. E. fide
of Guadaloupe, of which the wefternmoft is called Terre de Bas,
or the Low Ifland; the eafternmoft the High Ifland: there is a
good harbour here for a few fhips.   Thefe iflands received the
name of Sanctos from the Spaniards, who firft difcovered them
on All Saints day.   There is fome good land in the valleys, but
the hills are covered with rocks.—Thus, in the fhort period of
three months, concluded a campaign, in which three valuable
iflands and their dependencies were added to his majefty's dominions.   To the unanimity which fubfifted between the Commanders in Chief, together with their allowed high profeffional
knowledge, and feconded by the fpirited conduct of all the inferior ranks, muft this unlooked-for fuccefs be attributed, as the
force employed to effect it was certainly far fhort of what it ought
to have been for fo great an enterprife.   The originally fmall army
was now obliged to be divided, to garrifon and fecure our newly-

acquired poffeffions; the fatigue became the more burthenfome,
and the troops that had gone through the campaign with unexampled bravery and patience, at length began to feel the effects
of a climate, that even in peaceable times is often found too try-
ing for European conftitutions; and which was at this period rendered tenfold more fevere by that dreadful malady the yellow fever, which, though it had fubfided when we firft came to the Weft
Indies, was now, as it were, awakened by the arrival of frefh victims, and acquired more ftrength from the fmall refiftance that
could be made againft it by conftitutions already broken by fatigue
under hardfhips and difficulties unparalleled.— As there were
no expectations of any reinforcements of confequence being fent
till November, the General determined to return to England,
after he had made a proper arrangement to render the conquefts
permanent, and fecure them againft any attempt that might be
made by thofe perturbed fpirits that, notwithftanding his utmoft
vigilance, might remain in the colonies; and which he in a fhort
time effected to his fatisfaction, fo far as it related to any attempt
that could be made by the enemy in thefe parts: but it is not to
be imagined that, with the fmall number of men he originally
brought out, now reduced by a variety of caufes to half their
number, and daily decreafing in an alarming degree, any refiftance
could be made againft a ftrong reinforcement, if the French nation fhould be able to fend out one, from Europe[1].   Previous to

[1] After the iflands were captured, a fmall reinforcement arrived, which was to be retained by Sir Charles
Grey, if he thought fit; but as he knew it was much wanted to carry on the war at St. Domingo, and as it

his return, however, he was determined to leave the iflands in the beft poffible ftate of defence; and for that purpofe he, with the Admiral, vifited all the iflands in this quarter, infpecting the ftrong pofts and fortifications, while the Admiral paid attention to the naval department in each; and in the beginning of June, after having taken formal leave of the army in general orders, he failed for Europe.

was infufficient to enable him to undertake an expedition againft Cayenne, which he at firft intended, he fent it on to Jamaica, under the command of Brigadier General Whyte; and Lieutenant Colonel Lennox, who came out foon after, he difpatched thither alfo.

CHAPTER XI.

THE CHARGES OF EXTORTED CONTRIBUTIONS AND OPPRESSIONS, ALLEDGED AGAINST THE COMMANDERS IN CHIEF BY CERTAIN INTERESTED INDIVIDUALS, REFUTED.... THE REAL CAUSES OF THE LOSS OF GUADALOUPE.

AFTER having given an account of the glorious fuccefs which had crowned the exertions of our gallant commanders and their forces, I now enter upon a lefs pleafant tafk, the lofs of Guadaloupe, fince followed by the capture of fome other iflands: but I do it the more willingly, becaufe in the fimple facts it will be my duty to detail, the real caufe of thofe misfortunes will apppear, and a clear refutation enfue of thofe grofs calumnies, originally propagated by avarice, fraud, and falfehood, and repeated by ignorance and malice, which have endeavoured to fix a ftigma on two commanders, whofe integrity of heart and opennefs of conduct are as demonftrable, as their bravery is acknowledged.

The accufation of plunder, confifcation, and *extorted contribution*, is founded on a tale, of which half only has been told, and that half with intentional inaccuracy.

It has always been underftood that property found in any place taken by ftorm or affault became the legal prize or booty of

the captors; confequently the Commanders in Chief found no he-
fitation or difficulty in confidering the produce, merchandife, &c.
afloat and on fhore at St. Pierre and Fort Royal (both which were
literally fo taken) as juftly liable to forfeit and confifcation. The
eftates of the emigrant royalifts had been fequeftered, and the
produce of them fold by the agents of the republic; confequently
all manufactured or collected produce on them became in like
manner, by his majefty's gracious bounty, the right of the captors.

If what is found in places or veffels taken by affault be not
confidered as legal prize, what is? Is no booty, no prize money,
to be the reward of fuccefsful heroifm, after the dreadful fatigues,
difeafes, and dangers of war? Where then will be the fpur to noble
actions? Where the fpirit that impels the foldier and the failor
to brave the horrors of arms and elements, of raging ficknefs, of
excruciating death?

All the produce and merchandife found in the town of Fort
Royal and on board the veffels in the Carénage, and the fame in
the town and bay of St. Pierre and in Trinité in the ifland of
Martinique, and at Baffe Terre and Point à Pitre in Guadaloupe,
were difpofed of by public auction for the benefit of the captors:
but thofe on the eftates, manufactured and packed ready to be
brought down to the ports for embarkation, were not fold at this
time, becaufe perfons came forward on the part of the inhabitants
themfelves, and propofed a contribution, in lieu of that part of
the property, as falling more eafy on them, and confequently being preferable to confifcation; though they did not at that time

pretend to difpute the legality of the forfeiture. The Commanders in Chief acceded to this *their own propofal*, through a pure wifh of accommodation. The exorbitant and unprecedented contribution, therefore, levied on an unwilling people, turns out to be an *offered compromife for an undifputed prize, received by a merciful and tender conqueror out of kindnefs to the conquered.*

How well beftowed this kindnefs was, how deferved the confidence placed in the honour of thefe people, will appear by the fequel! They received back the forfeitures, and then endeavoured to get rid of paying the compromife (themfelves had offered) by infamous mifreprefentations of the conduct of thofe Commanders, of whofe generofity they made ufe, to defame, and then to rob them! For no fooner had they fhipped off the property, and got it fafe away from the power of the Commanders, than they began to demur at paying the ftipulated fum, particularly at St. Lucia, which ifland had agreed to pay one hundred and fifty thoufand pounds.

Situated as I was, and having an opportunity of drawing my conclufions on the fpot, I venture, with a very ftrong confidence of its truth, to relate the following as the fecret hiftory of this bufinefs. An agent for the prizes at St. Lucia, joining one of the agents who had already been employed in the fale of the vendible property at Martinique (poffibly piqued by fome diminution of confidence which the Commanders in Chief from good reafon had betrayed towards them), no fooner met the inhabitants of St. Lucia, whom he had convened on the fubject of raifing the ftipulated

P

compromife for the plunder, than he offered, with an unparalleled duplicity, while confeffing himfelf fent on the part of the captors, to fuggeft a mode by which the payment of this debt of honour might be evaded. "Send," faid he, "an immediate deputation "to the Englifh government, anticipate the ftory of the Com- "manders, and a prohibition will inftantly iffue." The deputation was fent without lofs of time: they relied on fecuring a large body of Englifh merchants, particularly thofe in the Weft Indies, on their fide; and their reliance was well placed, for they relied on that which they could eafily prove to be their intereft. The truth is, that many of thefe Weft India traders[r] had carried on an illicit traffic to the French iflands before they were captured; and in confequence of it had at the time of the capture immenfe fums ftill due to them. Apprehending, therefore, that the payment of this contribution might retard, or even endanger, the difcharge of their own debts, they joined heartily in every fcheme for defeating this juft and prior claim. They encouraged the French in their oppofition; they mifreprefented the facts to England; they attempted to blaft the laurels of the Commanders; and became clamorous againft the cruelty of plunder, and illegality and impolicy of confifcation, that they might enjoy the rewards of their own treafon. While this plot was fecretly carrying on, and a heavy ftorm brooding over their heads, the General and Admiral were proceeding in their expedition againft Guadaloupe, little fuf-

---

[r] Admiral Rodney ufed to fay of thefe people, that "they were fmugglers in peace, and traitors in war;" an opinion, I believe, confirmed by repeated experience.

picious, till the difpatches from England difcovered the fuccefs with which the artful ftories of this party had been attended.

Thus was the unparalleled good order and difcipline with which the army and navy had abftained from plundering the towns of St. Pierre, Fort Royal, and Trinité, &c. rewarded! This was the recompence of the ruinous and expenfive fervice in which the officers had engaged; of the unexampled fufferings and dangers which they and their brave men had undergone. Is not contribution in lieu of booty, the cuftom of war? Was it not the cafe with Prince Ferdinand in a former war, through every town and village of Germany⁵? Did not the Marquis de Bouillé levy a heavy contribution on the ifland of St. Chriftopher's, when taken by the French in 1782? Where then could contribution ever be proper if not here? Here was no capitulation; but, though the iflands fell by ftorm, the Commanders, acting on the pureft principles, to fave the perfons and property of the inhabitants from the plunderᵗ of an enraged foldiery, agreed to accept as a recompence due to the forbearance and good conduct of that body, a

---

* Of this General Sir Charles Grey himfelf fhared.

t During the time that Fort Bourbon was befieging we fent a fummons to the town of St. Pierre, which was rejected with an uncommon degree of infolence, and Captain Mafon (the General's aid de camp, who went with the flag of truce) was infulted. About a fortnight afterwards the place was taken by ftorm, without any capitulation, confequently fubject to plunder by the cuftom of war; but fo far from any irregularity being fuffered, a drummer was hanged by order of General Dundas for attempting it; and fuch exact difcipline and quiet behaviour was maintained among the troops, that the fhops were opened the day after the capture. From the time of the refufal of the fummons to the final capture, the republicans continued to load all the property and produce on board veffels under American colours, which they did conftantly, in order to deprive the captors of their juft rights, in cafe the place fhould be taken.—Interefted American merchants were continually endeavouring to wreft the hard-earned prize money from the army and navy, while they were fupplying the enemy with provifions and other neceffaries.

compofition the moft eafy to the conquered; and yet their fame has been vilified, and the hard-earned pittance of booty fnatched away! for none of the contributions were ever paid, except a part at St. Lucia, *which was afterwards refunded.* Surely this is fmall encouragement for fuch a defperate fervice! If fuch be the future profpects of our army and navy, their fpirits will droop, and half that ardour that generates fuccefs fubfide!

I fhall now mention the real caufe of the lofs of Guadaloupe, which, with that of fome other iflands that have fince fallen, has been malicioufly attributed to the oppreffion and peculations of Sir Charles Grey and Sir John Jervis; for this purpofe I muft re-fer back to the time when the expedition was firft planned by our government, and the command given to thofe officers. As the capture of the French poffeffions in the Weft Indies was rightly judged to be of the greateft confequence both in a political and mercantile view, a very formidable armament was prepared, and Martinique was pitched on as the firft object for attack; and, fince the capture of that ifland had been attempted the year preceding, and failed, it was of courfe expected to be put on its guard, and rendered thereby more difficult. But at this period (unfortu-nately for this expedition) another object diverted the attention of government, and eight regiments", with a great part of the ar-tillery, which were embarked and ready to fail, were taken from that force, which combined would in all probability have fecured to us our conquefts in the Weft Indies, and enabled us to extend

" Confifting of four thoufand fix hundred and forty-two men.

them to St. Domingo, and all the other French iflands in that quarter. Government was well aware, and acknowledged, that this diminution of force muft fo cripple the expedition, that it would render the profpect of any fuccefs doubtful; and no idea was entertained that the conqueft of Martinique would even have been attempted, Fort Bourbon alone feeming too formidable for an attack by fuch an inconfiderable body: however, when Sir Charles Grey and Sir John Jervis arrived at Barbadoes, and had arranged every thing for an active campaign, they determined to begin with the ftrongeft ifland, being confident that, when that was gained, the fmaller places would foon fall; whereas, by attacking the leffer iflands firft, they muft neceffarily diminifh their fmall armament, and render the capture of fo well defended and ftrong a place as Martinique, with the formidable fortrefs of Fort Bourbon, totally impoffible. The event juftified their determination. But when this great object was gained, and St. Lucia and Guadaloupe taken, the army (originally too fmall) was divided into three parts to garrifon the conquered places; and by that dreadful fcourge, the yellow fever, which now began its ravages, together with the lofs fuftained in the feveral actions of the campaign, not one of the iflands, nor indeed a fingle poft on each, could be called properly defended, in cafe the French fhould fend out an armament to the Weft Indies. If, as foon as the news of the capture of the firft ifland had reached England, a ftrong reinforcement could have been fent out, and repeated on the conqueft of each fucceeding place, the fmall body of the enemy (who made their attack on Guadaloupe, and ſtole in at a moment when the gallant governor, General Dundas, was breathing his laſt, and when every poſt was reduced to extremity by ſickneſs) would with eaſe have been repelled, or perhaps their whole party taken.—In the ſucceeding part of this work it will be my buſineſs to detail the events that gradually led to the evacuation of this iſland, and gave the enemy ſuch advantage as enabled them ſince to extend their conqueſts to ſome other inferior places.

C. Willyams del.   J. Allen ſculpt.

Entrance of the Harbour of Point a Pitre.

CHAPTER XII.

GENERAL DUNDAS DIES OF THE YELLOW FEVER .... HIS CHA-
RACTER .... A FRENCH SQUADRON ARRIVES IN THE WEST
INDIES, AND TAKES POSSESSION OF GRAND TERRE .... THE
COMMANDERS IN CHIEF, ON RECEIVING AN ACCOUNT THERE-
OF, RETURN TO GUADALOUPE .... SIR CHARLES GREY LANDS
ON GRAND TERRE, AND TAKES THE HEIGHTS OF MASCOT. ...
SEVERAL ACTIONS TAKE PLACE .... A TRUCE TO BURY THE
DEAD .... AN UNSUCCESSFUL ATTACK ON POINT A PITRE.

On the evening of the 3d of June, Major General Thomas Dundas, the governor of Guadaloupe, became the victim of that dreadful fever, which once more began to defolate thefe iflands. He
was ill only three days. By his death the army in the Weft Indies fuffered an irreparable lofs, and the fervice in general one of
its brighteft ornaments. Amiable both in public and private life,
brave and generous, poffeffed of that true courage which never
exceeds the bounds of humanity, he juftly gained the love of the
army, and fell lamented by all that knew him[v]. At this inaufpi-

He was interred on the 4th of June, with all military honours, on one of the higheft batteries in Fort
Matilda, which, from that circumftance, was called Dundas's battery, and a ftone with a fuitable infcription
was placed over his remains. The command of the forces, and the government of Guadaloupe, now devolved
on Lieutenant Colonel Blundell of the forty-fourth regiment.

cious moment an armament arrived from France, under the direction of two commiſſioners from the national aſſembly. It conſiſted of two frigates, one corvette, two forty-fours armed en flute, and two other ſhips, with about one thouſand five hundred land forces on board of them ^w. They inſtantly made good their landing on Grand Terre; and, after two unſucceſsful efforts, at laſt ſucceeded in their attack on Fort Fleur d'Epée, which they carried by ſtorm^x.—As ſoon as this news reached Colonel Blundell, he inſtantly diſpatched a ſchooner to St. Chriſtopher's, with an account of it to the Commanders in Chief, which fortunately found them there, the Boyne being off Old Road taking in water for her voyage to England. Sir Charles Grey was buſy in inſpecting the works on Brimſtone Hill. The Commanders in Chief inſtantly determined to return to Guadaloupe, and accordingly puſhed, under a preſs of ſail, for Baſſe Terre, where they arrived in the

^w This armament appears to have ſailed from Rochfort about the 25th of April, and to have been forty-one days on the paſſage.

^x Their ſucceſs appears to have been greatly accelerated by the treachery or cowardice of ſeveral French royaliſts then in the fort, who offered their ſervices to ſally on the beſiegers. Accordingly they marched out; but, on approaching the enemy, they were panic ſtruck and fled, and few of them returned to Fleur d'Epée. The Britiſh merchants and ſailors from the town of Point à Pitre had thrown themſelves into this fort to aſſiſt the garriſon, which was greatly reduced by ſickneſs and death. This little band, under command of Lieutenant Colonel Drummond of the forty-third regiment, did all that gallant men could do; twice they repulſed the aſſailants; but at length, overpowered by numbers, and the royaliſts having demanded that the gates ſhould be thrown open, and the enemy now pouring in from all ſides, the few remaining troops were obliged to make the beſt retreat they could to Point à Pitre, which, not being tenable after the loſs of Fleur d'Epée, was abandoned by them, and they croſſed over to Baſſe Terre. In this affair, beſides the loſs of many others, Captain Suckling of the artillery was wounded at his gun by a bayonet, and left behind at Point à Pitre.—There were in Guadaloupe when taken by the French a larger proportion of troops than in either of the other conquered iſlands.

afternoon of the 7th of June, and were joined by the Refource, Captain Rofs, and the Winchelfea, Captain Lord Garlies; on board of which fhips General Grey and his fuite embarked to be landed at Baffe Terre, in order to vifit the ports in that quarter, and to give the neceffary inftructions for future operations. The Admiral ordered the Nautilus, Captain Bayntun, to proceed to Martinique, with orders from Sir Charles Grey for a reinforcement from thence, and himfelf proceeded in the Boyne to the Bay of Point à Pitre. On his paffage he met Commodore Thompfon with his fquadron from Martinique, coming round the point of Vieux Port. On their joining, he ordered the Solebay and Avenger into Baffe Terre Road, to carry the General's further orders into execution, touching reinforcements from the different iflands.

At noon of the 8th of June, the Boyne and the reft of the fleet anchored off Grozier, and faw the union jack difplayed on Fort Fleur D'Epée as a decoy to Britifh veffels, which we found had been fuccefsful in feveral inftances; from hence, too, we had a view of the French fleet lying in the harbour of Point à Pitre. The Admiral, without delay, arranged every thing in his department to prevent a furprife from any future reinforcements of the enemy which might arrive. At day-break of the 9th, the enemy in Fort Fleur d'Epée, on hoifting their colours, opened an heavy fire of round and grape-fhot on the Boyne, as did the two-gun battery at Grozier on the reft of the fleet, but happily without any material damage to them. This morning the London tranfport, having troops on board, got on fhore on the Baffe Terre fide of the bay. Lieutenant Thompfon of the Boyne, was fent with the launch to take the men out of her; in doing which he was expofed to a fevere fire from a battery on Iflet a Couchon, or Hog Ifland; but he fucceeded in removing them without any lofs. In the evening Sir Charles Grey and his fuite came on board the Boyne,ʸ from whence he could for the prefent with greater eafe arrange his troops, and communicate with them at their different pofts. This day alfo Lord Vifcount Garlies in the Winchelfea frigate attacked the two-gun battery at Grozier, where he had diftinguifhed himfelf in the laft campaign, and once more drove the enemy from their guns: but very few troops having yet arrived, no attempt could be made to land there, as before. The Boyne having been much annoyed by the fire of Fort Fleur d'Epeé and Grozier battery, was now warped a cable's length further from the fhore. On the 11th, in the morning, feveral boats full of men, attended by a gun-boat, were difcovered making towards our poft at Petit Bourg, from the harbour of Point à Pitre : their intention feemed to be to attack a tranfport and floop of ours. The Winchelfea frigate was ordered towards them, and receiving the fire of the battery on Hog ifland, and another near Fort Louis, fhe obliged them to return into the har-

ʸ Accompanied alfo by the Honourable Captain Stewart, brother to Lord Garlies; who having received permiffion to return to England, handfomely came forward at this time to offer himfelf as a volunteer.

In this fecond campaign (fee Appendix, page 37) Colonel Symes, Colonel Francis Dundas, and Colonel Sir Charles Gordon, were promoted to the rank of brigadier general.

bour. The enemy had croffed the river Sallée to Baffe Terre, and had taken poft at Berville, a fine plantation belonging to a gentleman of that name. They inftantly fet fire to the houfe, and deftroyed all the mills, fugar-works, and ftore-houfes, belonging to it, to a very large amount; they then encamped at the poft of St. Jean, or Gabbare, a point of land oppofite to the harbour of Point à Pitre. General Grey thought this a favourable moment to attack them, which was accordingly done at eleven o'clock at night on the 13th, under the command of Brigadier General Dundas, who with the 1ft light infantry led by Brevet Major Rofs, with the 39th regiment under Major Magan, and a de-detachment of artillery and two field-pieces, attacked the enemy with fuch determined bravery, that after a fevere conflict they fled in the utmoft diforder, precipitating themfelves into the fea in order to fwim acrofs the harbour to Point à Pitre; but few fuc-ceeded in the defperate attempt, many being drowned, and more fhot by our light infantry, who followed clofe at their heels: they left one hundred and feventy-nine dead on the field; our lofs was trifling, feven men killed and twelve wounded. The enemy's camp, colours, baggage, and ammunition, with one piece of cannon, fell into our hands.[z]   The light infantry and the 39th regiment remained at Berville, having for their advanced poft Savonge, and St. Jean on the banks of the river Sallée. On this point of land, which runs into the harbour of Point à Pitre, Captain Pratt, com-manding a detachment of artillery, was ordered to erect a battery

[z] See the Appendix, page 32.

of two twenty-four pounders and two howitzers, which he effected with fuch difpatch, that by the next morning it was completed, and opened with a moft tremendous fire on the republican frigate La Pique, lying within gunfhot of the fhore, to the no fmall furprife and aftonifhment of the commodore, who was then on board. The frigate retaliated, and a brifk fire was kept up for fome time, when fhe thought it advifable to weigh anchor, and take fhelter under the guns of her own batteries, after having loft between forty and fifty of her crew in killed and wounded, and being much damaged in her hull and rigging. On the 14th the Roebuck, Captain Chriftie, arrived with troops (draughted from feveral regiments), and two gun-boats alfo came very feafonably ; one of which, under command of Lieutenant Wolley of the Boyne, attacked the battery at Grozier, and again made the enemy retire from their guns.[a]

On Thurfday the 19th of June, General Grey once more made good his landing on Grand Terre, about fix miles to windward of Grozier, under cover of the Vanguard, Veteran, Vengeance, Solebay, and Winchelfea, and immediately moved on to Grozier, from whence he drove the enemy, who retreated towards Fort Fleur d'Epée, burning the houfes and fugar-works that lay in their

[a] On the 18th of June, Lieutenant Colonels Coote and Cradock arrived from St. Chriftopher's, where they had been detained by the yellow fever, which they had caught on board a tranfport in which they were proceeding to England on leave of abfence, and though not recovered from the baneful effects of that difeafe, they now came forward to offer their fervices to the Commanders in Chief, which were accepted in a manner highly honourable to both parties.

road.[b]   About this time Lieutenant Macnamara, of the marines, was fent to Defeada to fecure that ifland againft any attempt of the enemy. On his landing he was attacked by a party of the inhabitants, who had formerly furrendered the ifland to us, aided by fome brigands and a mixed rabble. In a fhort time, however, he drove them to the mountains, having killed twelve, and hung up fix, as an example to deter others from fimilar acts of rebellion. On the 20th the enemy funk one of our gun-boats by the fire of their battery on Hog Ifland, but none were killed in her. On the 21ft they fet fire to, and burnt a fine houfe on the heights of Mafcot, near Fleur d Epée, leaving the foundation walls only ftanding. Our troops now encamped at Grozier were employed in erecting batteries againft Fort Fleur d'Epée, as the enemy were in too great force for our reduced numbers to attempt an affault on their principal work. On the 22d the Honourable Captain Stewart, commanding the 9th grenadiers, and a party of feamen under Lieutenant Wolley,[c] marched from Grozier to attack St. Ann's Fort, a ftrong poft about twelve or fourteen miles to windward. After a moft fatiguing march, during which fome heavy fhowers of rain rendered the roads hardly paffable, they reached the foot of the hill on which the fort was fituated; up which our people fcrambled fo leifurely, and fuch a profound filence reigned

[b] In the afternoon one hundred and eighty feamen from the Boyne, Commanded by Lieutenants Wolley, Thomfon, and Maitland, landed under the Salines to windward of Grozier, and took poft on the heights near that place; other parties of feamen alfo were landed at Grozier, forming altogether a ftrong reinforcement for the army.

[c] With whom on this occafion Lieutenant Thomfon ferved as a volunteer.

among them, that they approached within fifteen or twenty paces of the centinel before he perceived them, though he was apparently alert on his poſt. Our French guide was now ſo terrified that he fired his piſtol at the centinel, which gave the alarm; inſtantly our troops ruſhed forward, and with three cheers began to ſtorm the works. The enemy were completely ſurpriſed, and not more than two of them eſcaped. During this the French emigrants who had accompanied our people, had marched into the town, where they began the moſt brutal exceſſes; but the humane exertions of our officers ſoon put a ſtop to their miſchievous proceedings. In this attack near four hundred of the enemy were killed, and one priſoner taken: on our part one only was wounded. Several ſloops and ſchooners were found in the bay, all in ballaſt and their ſails unbent, except one of them, in which Lieutenant Thomſon was ſent with an account of their ſucceſs to the Commanders in Chief. It being impoſſible to keep poſſeſſion of this poſt, from the ſmall number of our troops, and intelligence being brought that a large detachment of the enemy were on their march to cut off the retreat of this party, it was determined to return to the camp without loſs of time, all the ammunition having been previouſly deſtroyed, and the guns of the fort diſmounted.—The day proving unuſually hot, and the roads being deep and ſlippery from the inceſſant rains that had fallen during the preceding night, the troops were not able to reach the camp without halting; in conſequence of which they took poſt at a planter's houſe on an eminence, where they were received with great hofpitality. By three in the afternoon the men who had dropped down by the way from fatigue, were brought in (except two who reached the camp next morning), and the party proceeded to their different ftations without further accidents.[d]

On Tuefday the 24th of June, General Grey opened his batteries, which he had erected near Grozier, againft Fleur d'Epée; at the fame time Brigadier General Dundas kept up a fmart fire on Point à Pitre, where the enemy feemed to be making preparations againft the hurricane months, now approaching, by ftripping the fhips in the harbour of their fails and rigging. On the 26th, early in the morning, the enemy, to the number of three hundred, made a fortie from Fleur d Epée, on our advanced poft, confifting of one hundred men, but were foon obliged to retreat; we loft one man killed and eight wounded: at the fame time our batteries and gun-boats cannonaded the fort;

[d] In this bufinefs Lieutenant Wolley had fome narrow efcapes. The commanding officer of the fort rufhed out of the guard-room on the alarm, with a lighted match in his hand. He firft fired an amuzet, luckily pointed in an oppofite direction; he then three times attempted to fire a twenty-four pounder as Mr. Wolley and his men were advancing to the muzzle of it; but fortunately, either from the dampnefs of the powder, or trepidation of the man, it miffed taking effect; on which he flung down his match, and retreated to the further end of the fort, whither Mr. Wolley followed; but, from the darknefs of the night, he foon loft fight of him. As he returned he was met by his own men, who, taking him for an enemy, were about to put him to death, when his voice difcovered their miftake. Had the cannon in the firft inftance gone off, it muft have made confiderable havock among our men, as it was loaded with a bag of mufket balls.—This day Captain Armftrong of the 8th regiment, was killed by a cannon ball at the landing-place at Grozier, while giving directions to a ferjeant about fome ordnance which was to be landed there. He was on horfeback, and had juft remarked, that there could be no danger from the fire at Fleur d'Epée at that place; a fhot, however, from the fort dipped over the point of land which feemed to fhelter the landing-place, and cut him afunder. He has often been heard to fay that he thought that a man muft be truly unfortunate who fell by a fingle cannon ball.

in the latter two feamen were wounded. On the 27th, the batteries at Grozier having opened as ufual on Fleur d'Epée, a detachment of our troops under Brigadier General Fifher marched forward to attack a piquet of the enemy pofted on Morne Mafcot, from whence they drove them after a fharp conteft, and eftablifhed themfelves, as our advanced poft, within mufket fhot of the fort.ᵉ During the preceding night the light infantry at camp Berville were fent by Brigadier General Dundas, under command of Major Rofs of the 25th regiment, to Petit Bourg, where they embarked, and joined the army at Grozier. This movement, by which the main body was much ftrengthened, was effected unperceived by the enemy, and the 39th and 43d regiments only left at Berville.

Several fkirmifhes now daily took place, and many fell on both fides; though, from want of fteadinefs at the laft, the enemy were always greater lofers than ourfelves. On the morning of the 29th of June, a large body of the enemy, to the number of one thoufand, marched out of Fort Fleur d'Epée, and feemed to meditate an attack on a detachment of light infantry under Colonel Gomm, pofted to the right of the grenadiers who were on Morne Mafcot, under Brigadier General Fifher. By this falfe

ᵉ In this affair Captain Morrifon of the 58th regiment was killed by a mufket ball through his head as he was leading his men on to the attack; he fell regretted by all who knew him, being an accomplifhed, amiable, and brave man: I too felt feverely on this occafion, having enjoyed much of his fociety and friendfhip. The Commander in Chief, who knew his worth, paid the tribute of applaufe to his memory; and the Admiral when he heard of his fall, exclaimed, "He has left few equals behind him."

movement, they hoped that a detachment of the grenadiers would be fent to reinforce the light infantry, and thereby weaken the force on Morne Mafcot, which was their real object of attack. In a fhort time, however, they were perceived mounting the fide of Mafcot heights, with colours flying and finging the national fongs, covered by a heavy fire of round and grape-fhot from Fleur d'Epée, which prevented our grenadiers from fhewing themfelves till the enemy were clofe to them; on which General Fifher made them proftrate themfelves on the ground, and wait the approach of the enemy in that pofture. The inftant the republicans came within a few yards of them they ftarted up, and an obftinate engagement commenced, which terminated at length by the grenadiers advancing to the charge; on which the enemy fled, and were purfued down the hill with great flaughter. Our lofs amounted to thirty killed and wounded: among the former was Lieutenant Toofey of the 65th regiment; of the latter, Captain De Rivigne of the artillery, received a ball in the fide of his neck. Brigadier General Fifher was hit three times by grape-fhot, which caufed contufions only, and his horfe was killed under him. In the evening the enemy fent in a flag of truce, requefting permiffion to bury their dead and carry off their wounded, which was granted them;[f] yet they left a number of both, on the fide of the

---

[f] A young officer, formerly of Walfh's regiment, took this opportunity of efcaping to us. His name was Clarke, his family of Martinique, where his father was a counfellor at law. He had been imprifoned three months at Bourdeaux, on his endeavouring to avoid joining the armies on the frontiers, and was releafed to embark on this expedition, as the only chance of rejoining his friends. He reported, that one Fremont, a daring fellow, who, though not firft in command, had great influence, was killed this morning on the

hill, to the great annoyance of our piquet, which during the following night was disturbed by the groans of the dying and wounded. The day following the enemy again made an attempt, in equal force, against our post on Mascot, and was again repulsed with great loss. The rainy season being already set in, and the hurricane months now approaching, determined the Commander in Chief to make an effort to finish the campaign at once. From his success in the two last engagements, and the excellent manner in which he had planned the attack, it would no doubt have succeeded, had his orders been punctually obeyed. The plan he had laid down was, for a large body of troops under General Symes, to march during the night, and make themselves masters of Morne Government, and the other commanding heights round the town of Point à Pitre, whilst himself, at the head of the rest of his army, was in readiness on the heights of Mascot to storm Fort Fleur d'Epée, on receiving a signal from General Symes; but, from some unfortunate misapprehension, the whole of General Grey's well-concerted plan was rendered abortive, and the almost total destruction of our exhausted forces ensued: but it is my business to detail the events of this unfortunate affair as accurately as the confused accounts I have received will permit. Brigadier General Symes, having under his command the first battalion of grena-

walls of Fleur d'Epée, by a musket-ball from one of our people. The enemy lost in this action upwards of three hundred men. On the 29th, the Commander in Chief sustained a heavy loss in the death of Captain Newton Ogle, of the 70th regiment, one of his excellency's aid-de-camps; he was a young man of an excellent understanding, and had distinguished himself on all occasions where his exertions had been called forth.

diers, commanded by Brigadier General Fifher, and the firft and fecond light infantry, led by Colonel Gomm, with a detachment of feamen from the Boyne^g and Veteran, commanded by Captain Robertfon of the Veteran, marched from the heights of Mafcot at about nine o'clock at night, on the 1ft of July. They firft defcended into a deep ravine thick planted with coffee bufhes, through which there was no road, the feamen bringing up the rear. The night was uncommonly dark, which rendered their march both dangerous and fatiguing After proceeding about a mile they halted on a road, and were joined by two fmall field-pieces, which were put under the charge of Lieutenants Thomfon and Maitland, to be dragged by their feamen. During the halt fome people, who were heard to fpeak French, were feen near the rear; Lieutenant Wolley endeavoured to fecure them, but they efcaped through the bufhes, and no further notice was taken of this. The army moved forward about two miles further, on a road leading through deep ravines, and made a fecond halt for about an hour; the march was then re-commenced, but no orders ever paffed during the time: they now proceeded for fome miles without meeting with any obftruction, when an order came for the feamen in the rear to advance to the attack, which they did by running as faft as they could for upwards of a mile. The parties they paffed were not in the beft order, owing to the quicknefs of the march, until they came to the grenadiers, who were

---

^g Lieutenant Wolley of the Boyne, was appointed acting major of brigade; and Lieutenants Thomfon and Maitland, and Mr. Ofwald, commanded the three companies of feamen.

drawn up as a corps de referve. About this time the bugle horn founded to advance, and foon after a heavy firing of round and grape-fhot from Morne Government, and alfo from feveral other batteries of the enemy, commenced, as alfo from fome twelve-pounders landed from the fhipping in the harbour, which were placed in tiers, and entirely enfiladed the road along which the troops were advancing. After paffing the grenadiers, the feamen were halted for a few minutes to form, they being perfectly out of order from running; but fcarce thirty of them were got to-gether, when Lieutenant Wolley was ordered to advance with them, and Captain Robertfon remained to form and bring up the reft. The cannonading from the enemy's guns was the moft fe-vere the oldeft foldier ever witneffed, efpecially from the guns which were on the road; two or three tiers of which were planted behind each other, from which the enemy were driven by the bayonets of our gallant fellows, who no fooner had taken one battery, but another opened on them from behind. The whole now became a fcene of confufion impoffible to defcribe. Inftead of any of the heights being attempted, the greater part of the troops and the feamen were got into the town, where they were mowed down by the grape-fhot, which played upon them in every direc-tion,[h] as well as mufketry from the windows of the houfes. Where-ever our men perceived this, they broke open the doors, putting

[h] One of the frigates in the harbour did great execution; by a fingle difcharge of grape-fhot, killing three officers and thirty-fix privates of the light infantry, who were unfortunately drawn up in a ftreet effectually commanded by her guns.

all they found in them to death; and thofe who could not ftand the bayonet were fhot as they leaped from the windows. General Symes was by this time badly wounded,[i] and his horfe killed under him. Colonel Gomm (who led the light infantry), with feveral other officers, was killed, and a great many more defperately wounded;[k] and Captain Robertfon, who commanded the feamen, was blown up. At length General Fifher (the fecond in command, who, as well as every other officer on this fervice, was ignorant of General Symes's plans) founded a retreat, and the miferable remains of this gallant party marched off, the enemy haraffing them in their retreat, though kept at bay by the gallant exertions of the Honourable Captain Stewart with a party of grenadiers, affifted by Lieutenant Wolley and the feamen of the Boyne, who covered the retreat; till at length the latter fell by a mufket-ball through his leg, and was brought off by his men. When the remains of this unfortunate detachment got back to Mafcot,[l] General Grey found it in vain to attempt any thing

[i] General Symes died foon after of his wound.

[k] Captain Burnet of the 43d regiment, who had led his company of grenadiers into the town, was blown up at the time Captain Robertfon was killed. His clothes being on fire, were pulled off by his brother officers. His face and hands were rendered entirely black by the explofion. In this fituation he firft received a mufket-ball which broke his arm, and was then met by his own grenadiers, who, taking him for one of the French blacks, attacked him with charged bayonets, and wounded him in three places before he could make himfelf known to them. The inftant they difcovered their miftake they expreffed the utmoft horror and contrition, and brought off this excellent officer in their arms; who, I am happy to be enabled to add, furvived, notwithftanding the dreadful fituation he was in. Lieutenant Conway of the 60th regiment, was alfo blown up, and in that condition continued to lead on his men and encourage them, till unfortunately he fell by a mufket-ball through his body.

[l] General Grey was waiting on Morne Mafcot for Brigadier General Symes's fignal of his having fucceeded in taking the heights near Point à Pitre; having the fecond battalion of grenadiers, the 65th regiment,

againſt Fleur d'Epée, being obliged to detach the ſecond battalion of grenadiers to cover the retreat, and his troops being all ſo much reduced and exhauſted, yet from the effect of the batteries he had erected to cover his attack of Fleur d Epée, which opened on that fort in the evening, there could have been no doubt of ſucceſs had not the above-related misfortune taken place.[m] It being totally impoſſible to attempt any thing further at this ſeaſon, the General that night began to reimbark his cannon and mortars, and in two days had got off the whole of his troops without loſs; he then ſtrengthened the poſts on Baſſe Terre, and having made the beſt arrangements poſſible to maintain them, and to enable him to renew his attacks on Point à Pitre and Fleur d'Epée after the hurricane months, in caſe any reinforcements ſhould arrive (without which it would be totally impoſſible), he embarked on board the Boyne, leaving Brigadier General Colin Graham to command on Baſſe Terre, and then repaired to St. Pierre in the iſland of Martinique, where he eſtabliſhed his head-quarters. The Boyne proceeded to Fort Royal Bay, where ſhe was laid up for the hurricane months in a ſnug harbour, called Trois Iſlet Bay, and the ſick and wounded were landed for the

and ſix companies of Grand Terre, and ſecond battalion of ſeamen commanded by Captain Sawyer, ready to attack Fort Fleur d'Epée by ſtorm.

[m] Our loſs in killed, wounded, and miſſing, amounted to thirty-eight officers, forty-three ſerjeants, and ſix hundred and eleven privates.

I muſt here beg leave to add an extract from Admiral Sir J. Jervis's public letters to the Lords of the Admiralty on this ſubject. " The fate of Captain Lewis Robertſon, who had diſtinguiſhed himſelf highly, fills my mind with the deepeſt regret; he had long been a child of misfortune, although he poſſeſſed talents benefit of frefh air, and every attention paid to them that could alleviate their fufferings.

to merit every fuccefs and profperity; and, as I am informed, has left a widow and infant family unprovided for. I beg leave to recommend them to the protection and good offices of their lordfhips, to obtain a fuitable provifion, which will be a great encouragement to officers in fimilar circumftances, to emulate fo great an example."

The celebrated Brigadier General Arnold, being on bufinefs of a mercantile nature at Point à Pitre, was cap- tured at the time the place fell into the hands of the republicans, and, being apprehenfive of ill treatment, changed his name to Anderfon. He was put on board a prifon-fhip in the harbour, and had confiderable property in cafh with him, of which, it is fuppofed, Fremont and Victor Hughes were informed, as he received an intimation from one of the French fentries, that he was known, and would foon be guillotined. On this alarming intelligence he determined to attempt an efcape, which he effected in the following maf- terly manner. At night he lowered into the fea a cafk containing clothes and valuables, with a direction on it, that if it floated to the fhore of our camp at Berville, it might be known, and reftored to him; he then lowered down his cloak bag to a fmall raft which he had prepared, on which alfo he got himfelf, and proceeded to a fmall canoe, in which he pufhed for the Britifh fleet, directed by the Admiral's lights. On his making towards the mouth of the harbour he was challenged by the French row guard, but by the darknefs of the night efcaped from them, and arrived on board the Boyne by four o'clock on Monday morning, the 30th of June.

During the whole time of this latter campaign the fever, which had been fo deftructive the preceding year, continued to rage in our army and navy with unabated violence. General Grey loft all the fervants he brought from England by it, including two who had lived with him for many years. It firft broke out with violence when the former campaign ended.

C Willyams del.   J Aiken fecit

Fleur d'Epée.

CHAPTER XIII.

THE COMMANDERS IN CHIEF SAIL TO MARTINIQUE . . . . PRO-
CEEDINGS THERE, AND AT GUADALOUPE . . . . . CAMP BER-
VILLE TAKEN . . . . OCCURRENCES THEREUPON . . . . GENERAL
PRESCOTT ENTERS FORT MATILDA, WHICH IS INVESTED BY
THE FRENCH . . . . SIR JOHN VAUGHAN AND ADMIRAL CALD-
WELL ARRIVE IN THE WEST INDIES . . . . SIR CHARLES GREY
AND SIR JOHN JERVIS RESIGN THEIR COMMAND, AND RE-
TURN TO EUROPE.

SIR Charles Grey, after giving the neceſſary orders for erecting
batteries to protect and ſecure the camp on Baſſe Terre, ſailed
with the Admiral to Martinique, and eſtabliſhed his head-quarters
at St. Pierre;[n] having previouſly diſtributed the troops (which

[n] Among the many cauſes of uneaſineſs that now bore hard upon the Commanders in Chief (by the failure
of their well-concerted plans, the dreadful mortality among their troops, and the deſpair of reinforcements arriving from Europe) the miſconduct of one high in eſtimation as an officer, and hitherto looked
upon as a man of ſtrict integrity, was not the leaſt galling. The caſe was this: At the taking of St. Lucia,
Colonel Sir Charles Gordon, who had repeatedly diſtinguiſhed himſelf by his gallant conduct, was appointed
governor of that iſland, and in the laſt promotion was advanced to the rank of brigadier general; ſoon after
which ſome very unpleaſant reports prevailed, of extortions and peculations by him, and taking bribes of the
inhabitants, who were ſuppoſed to be diſaffected, in order to ſuffer them to remain on the iſland, and then
breaking his word with them. At length a regular complaint was laid before the Commander in Chief,
who inſtantly ordered a court martial to be ſummoned, and ſent an officer to St. Lucia to arreſt Sir Charles
Gordon, and convey him to Martinique, in order for trial. At this time the fever raged ſo violently that

S

were not left under General Graham on Baſſe Terre) throughout the iſlands, where the Brigands began to be very troubleſome; and even at Martinique, where the Commander in Chief reſided, they had the audacity to ſhew themſelves, encouraged by the ſickneſs which raged in all quarters, and daily weakened our poſts. At Grande Rivere and Calabaſs they appeared in ſome force; on which the Commander in Chief detached Captain Hare, at the head of a detachment of the Prince of Wales's light ° dragoons, with Lieutenant Colonel De Soter and the iſland rangers, who attacked and routed them, taking three of their leaders priſoners, and diſperſing the reſt. At Guadaloupe no time was loſt by Brigadier General Graham in preparing both for attack and defence; he erected gun and mortar batteries upon the banks of the river Sallée, in the different ſituations where it was moſt likely the enemy might attempt to croſs it from Grande Terre; namely, at the gabarre or ferry, which heretofore was the point of communication between the two parts of the iſland; at Morne Savon and at St. Jean, both commanding the town of Point à Pitre and Morne Go-

the two firſt courts-martial that met on this buſineſs, were diſſolved by the death of a majority of the members. At length, in order to prevent the like accident from again interrupting the courſe of juſtice, the General appointed a greater number of officers than uſual to attend, and the trial proceeded; the event of which was, that the priſoner was found guilty of the crimes laid to his charge, and was ſentenced to refund the money he had extorted, and to be rendered incapable of ſerving his majeſty again: but, in conſequence of ſome favourable circumſtances that came out on the trial, he was allowed to ſell his commiſſion. See Appendix, pages 42, 43, 48.

° The horſes that were ſent from America for the purpoſe of mounting the light dragoons, were ſo bad, that only three out of forty were found, or fit for ſervice, inſomuch that Captain Hare was obliged to preſent a memorial to the Commander in Chief on the ſubject.

vernment. By thefe precautions the Commander in Chief hoped to prevent the enemy from croffing into Baffe Terre till he could get a reinforcement from England, which he had expected for fome time, and had now difpatched Brigadier General Francis Dundas to explain to government the abfolute neceffity there was for a fupply of troops in the conquered iflands. The head-quarters of the army in Guadaloupe were at Camp Berville, a very command-ing ground, flanked by the fea on one fide, and on the other by an impaffable fwamp and wood; about a league in front was the river Sallée, on the oppofite banks of which ftood the town of Point à Pitre; and at the rear, about a mile from the camp, was a narrow pafs, by which alone it could be approached. The bat-teries under the direction of Captain De Rivigne, deftroyed a great part of the town, fo that the inhabitants were obliged to evacuate it, and encamp on the adjacent hills. The baneful effects of the climate, together with the neighbouring fwamps, began now to be feverely felt by our army, the officers and men died daily in numbers, and by the middle of Auguft the lift of fick and conva-lefcents compofed by far the majority in the camp. Two frigates and two floops of war were ordered by the Admiral to cruize off the harbour of Point à Pitre, to prevent fupplies being carried to the enemy; notwithftanding which many American and other veffels from the neighbouring difaffected iflands, contrived to elude their vigilance. Victor Hughes, the commiffioner from the French convention, and now commander in chief of their troops in this ifland (the commanders of the army and navy that came out

with him being dead), was indefatigable in gaining over the blacks
and mulattoes to his intereft; and, in confequence of his late fuccefs, they flocked in great numbers to his ftandard. As they came
in he formed them into different corps, and had them inftructed
in the ufe of arms. The remains of the fecond battalion of grenadiers[p] were ordered about the latter end of Auguft to Guadaloupe, to relieve the flank companies of the 15th and 64th regiments: they embarked at Fort Royal on board the Dictator, and
landed at Petit Bourg, from whence they marched directly to the
camp. During the month of September the troops in the different camps were, from ficknefs, inadequate to furnifh guards for
the different batteries. Several companies could not produce a
fingle man fit for duty; the 43d could not afford a corporal and
three men at night, for the protection of their own camp, much
lefs give their complement for the batteries. The greater part of
the town of Petit Bourg was converted into hofpitals for our fick,
befides great numbers ill in the camps; the officers were equal
fufferers with the men, fo much fo, that field officers were obliged
to mount captain's guard. The different iflands were drained of
their troops, in order to keep up fome appearance in front of the
enemy; and the royalifts had taken the duty of the Gabarre for
fome time paft, where they conducted themfelves with much fpirit in feveral attacks made upon them by the enemy from the oppofite fide of the river. The grenadiers that arrived laft, were

Confifting of feventy rank and file only.

now reduced, in lefs than three weeks, to twenty men; and from the fituation of the feveral camps on the verge of the fwamps, a ground they were obliged to occupy, was truly deplorable. About this time General Prefcott arrived at the town of Baffe Terre, where he took the command, and no appearance of any reinforcement from England as yet cheered our drooping fpirits. On Saturday, the 26th of September, the enemy from Point à Pitre and Fort Louis embarked a large body of troops in fmall veffels, and paffing our fhips of war unperceived, under cover of the dark night, effected two different landings on Baffe Terre; the one at Goyave, to the eaftward of Petit Bourg, and the other at Lamantin, near Bay Mahault. As foon as it was known that this landing was effected, moft of our fick were carried from Petit Bourg on board the fhips that lay near that place, and when the news was received at head-quarters, General Graham ordered all the troops from the different camps to join at Berville, as the ftrongeft fituation. Every exertion was made to fortify this poft in the beft manner poffible: acrofs the narrow pafs by which alone it could be approached by land, a ftrong breaft-work was thrown up, with embrafures for fix field-pieces; on the flanks, and immediately in the rear of this, another was thrown up; and in front of both, on the brow of the hill, a ftrong abbatis was formed. The enemy that landed at Bay Mahault foon poffeffed themfelves of that place; they then marched on to the Gabarre, where they had nearly furrounded the royalifts before they were able to make their retreat to the camp. The poffeffion of the Gabarre afforded them

an eafy conveyance for guns, ammunition, cattle, &c. from Grande
Terre, and they now made their appearance in fight of our camp.
The enemy, who had landed on the oppofite part of the ifland, as
foon as day broke upon them, began their march to Petit Bourg.
Lieutenant Colonel Drummond of the 43d regiment, with fome
convalefcents from the hofpital, and a party of royalifts, advanced
to meet them; but perceiving their great fuperiority of numbers,
found it advifable to retreat through Petit Bourg, and took poft
at a battery upon the fhore called Point Bacchus, between that
village and Camp Berville. The enemy, on taking poffeffion of
Petit Bourg, exercifed the moft unheard of cruelties on the unfortunate fick in the hofpitals, putting all they found to death; fome
of them were fortunate enough to be taken off by the boats belonging to the men of war lying there. Too much praife cannot be
given to Captain Boyer q of the Affurance, for his humane exertions on this occafion. From the hofpitals to the wharf was a
continued fcene of mifery and horror, being ftrewed with the
bodies of the fick, who were barbaroufly put to death as they
were crawling to the fhore, in hopes of being taken off by our
boats. The next movement of the enemy was to Point Bacchus,
where Colonel Drummond and his party, being furrounded, were
made prifoners. The enemy keeping poffeffion of this poft, entirely cut off all communication between the camp and our fhipping. They then proceeded to poffefs themfelves of the fur-

q I am forry to add, that this officer foon afterwards fell a victim to the yellow fever.

rounding heights, and formed a junction with the other party which landed at Bay Mahault; by which Camp Berville was completely furrounded on the land fide. The utmoft ftrength of Berville camp was now about two hundred and fifty regular troops, and three hundred royalifts; but none of thefe could be called effective, being reduced to extremity by ficknefs and fatigue. The enemy inftantly began to form batteries, one of which, on an eminence, in fome meafure commanded our camp. On the 29th of September, in the morning, the enemy in a large body attacked our advanced work; our field-pieces and mufketry opened a heavy fire upon them, and an engagement enfued, which continued with equal fury for three hours; when, after having been charged the third time by our troops, the enemy retreated, leaving on the field in killed and wounded feven hundred men, our lofs amounting to about twenty. In the forenoon of this day, the enemy had fent a number of gun-boats from Point à Pitre, fome of which anchored off the fhore at Berville, and others under Point Bacchus, with a view to ftop the communication between our camp and fhipping, and force the latter out of the harbour of Petit Bourg. Each of their fchemes fucceeded, fo that now the camp (ill fupplied with provifions and ftores, which were left chiefly at Petit Bourg) faw no poffibility of getting a further fupply. This morning Major Irvine was killed by a twenty-four pounder from the enemy's gun-boat, as he was fitting in the cabin of the Affurance; in which he and a number of others had embarked. As foon as the news of thefe difafters reached the Commanders in Chief, the Boyne was got out of Trois Iflet Bay, without lofs of time; and, although the hurricane feafon was not entirely paft, the Admiral embarked, and failed on Tuefday, the 30th of Sep-tember, from Martinique, and anchored off Grozier, in the bay of Point à Pitre, by 10 A. M. On Thurfday, the 2d of October, the two-gun battery there, opened upon us with red-hot fhot, and continued to fire for a confiderable time, but without ef-fect. This night the Admiral endeavoured to open a communi-cation with Camp Berville, but was prevented by the vigilance of the enemy, who now occupied every avenue to it. On the morning of the 30th, the enemy renewed their attacks on Ge-neral Graham's camp at Berville, and again on the 4th of October, ftill bringing (hydra like) greater numbers to the charge; their fuccefs, however, was the fame as on the firft attack, having loft during the three attacks, on a moderate computation, two thoufand men. In the fecond attack General Graham was wounded by a mufket-ball in the leg, and feveral of his officers fell.[r] After the third action the enemy fent in a flag of truce, offering terms of capitulation, which General Graham in a fpirited

---

[r] In one of thefe attacks Monfieur Vermont was fhot through the body, his lieutenant, Monfieur De Lifle, was fhot through his breaft, and another of his officers killed; in this fituation he beat off the enemy. This gallant, but unfortunate officer, was, at the beginning of the revolution, poffeffed of a good eftate near Trois Riviere on Baffe Terre, which foon made him an object of republican vengeance; his houfe was at-tacked, but he efcaped into the woods, fuppofing that his amiable wife would be fafe from their fury, being far advanced in her pregnancy; but the monfters, not regarding her fituation, put her to death with cir-cumftances of barbarity too dreadful to relate, and fuch as would fill, I truft, every Briton's breaft with the utmoft horror; his aged mother too, and beautiful fifter, fhared the fame fate. He was taken and thrown into prifon at Fort Matilda, to referve him for a public fpectacle on the guillotine, when we arrived, and re-leafed him from thence by the capture of the ifland.

manner refufed; the officers, however, waited on the General, and
ftated, that the troops, reduced by ficknefs and fatigue, were no
longer able to undergo the duty, which now preffed heavy on
them, and were fo haraffed as to be incapable of withftanding another attack, which the enemy promifed to make on them the following morning. General Graham therefore, reconfidering the
matter, confented to fend a flag to the enemy, and, after fome
time, the terms of capitulation were agreed to; but, alas! the
unfortunate royalifts were not included, though the General endeavoured all he could to make terms for them: he fucceeded
however thus far, to have permiffion to fend a covered boat to
the Boyne, in which he embarked twenty-five officers of the
royalifts; their unfortunate brethren, to the number of three hundred, who had defended their pofts to the laft, with the moft determined refolution, were doomed to fuffer death by the hands of
their republican countrymen in cold blood, in a manner hitherto,
I believe, unheard of, at leaft unrecorded in the annals of the
moft favage and abandoned people.ˢ Humanity muft fhudder at
the idea; the republicans erected a guillotine, with which they
ftruck off the heads of fifty of them. Thinking, however, this mode

Their conduct prior to, and fince the enemy had attacked the camp, deferved a far better fate: finding
themfelves excluded from terms of capitulation, they wifhed permiffion to cut their way through the enemy's
army, by which a few of them, at leaft, might efcape, and the reft meet an honourable death; but this
requeft, it is faid, was refufed; perhaps it was believed that on their capture the enemy would relent, and
not put their fanguinary threats into execution. Two of thefe unfortunate men haftened to the fhore, in hopes
of getting on board the covered boat; but being difappointed, and aware of the fate that awaited them, they
inftantly fhot themfelves on the beach. On hearing of this melancholy bufinefs, General Grey publifhed an
order that did equal honour to his feelings and his mind. See Appendix, page 53.

T

of proceeding too tedious, they invented a more fummary plan; they tied the remainder of thefe unhappy men faft together, and placed them on the brink of the trenches which they had fo gallantly defended; they then drew up fome of their undifciplined recruits in front, who firing an irregular volley at their miferable victims, killed fome, wounded others, and fome, in all probability, were untouched; the weight however of the former dragged the reft into the ditch, where the living, the wounded, and the dead, fhared the fame grave, the foil being inftantly thrown upon them. The Englifh troops were to be allowed to march out with the honours of war, and to be embarked on board French fhips, which were to fail for England within twenty-one days after the furrender,[t] on condition that they would not ferve againft the French during the war. A great quantity of arms and ammunition fell into the hands of the enemy at this camp, and at Petit Bourg. Immediately after the furrender of Berville, Victor Hughes moved towards the town of Baffe Terre, now our laft ftake on this ifland, laying wafte the plantations, and burning the beautiful feats of the royalifts as he paffed along. Sir John Jervis, who had made every attempt to fuccour General Graham's camp at Berville, and had been an unwilling fpectator from the fleet, of the furrender of that camp to the enemy, now made fail for Baffe Terre, to render every affiftance in his power to

---

[t] This part of the agreement, however, was not complied with, as they remained prifoners for more than a year afterwards, during which time many of them died.

General Prefcott;^u and on the 9th of October, anchored within half a cable's length of the town. General Prefcott inftantly came on board to confult with the Admiral on the beft mode of procedure in this critical ftate of affairs; and it was determined that the whole force which the General could collect, fhould go into the fort, and the Admiral, in the Boyne, would render every affiftance in his power to the garrifon; a promife he performed in a manner that drew the warmeft thanks and approbation of General Prefcott and his officers. At this time the French royalifts had entirely abandoned us, and the militia, who had demanded arms, pofitively refufed to enter the fort, and foon after deferted to the enemy: a party in the town feemed alfo ready to rife upon our people; but by the vigilance and activity of General Prefcott they were overawed, and he continued to ride into the town un-attended as ufual. The fort was in a miferable ftate, nothing having been done to it fince the peace of 1783; and Clairfon-taine,^x a royalift, who had been appointed adminiftrateur general, wanting either influence or ability to procure negroes for the pur-

---

^u General Prefcott had fo fmall a force in that quarter, that he could not poffibly afford any material af-fiftance to General Graham; but he had made an effort by fending a detachment from the 35th regiment to fupport fome royalifts at St. Marié, which however proved ineffectual; and the numbers at Martinique being now too fmall for the defence of it, General Grey was unable to afford any affiftance from thence; how-ever he ordered the flank companies of the 4th battalion of the 60th regiment from St. Vincent's, and part of the 21ft from St. Chriftopher's, to reinforce Brigadier General Graham. Fortunately, however, they arrived too late, as their numbers were inadequate to fave it, and they afterwards made part of the garrifon at Fort Matilda.

^x This gentleman, after having enjoyed a lucrative poft, was unwilling to lofe the fruits of it, and, inftead of rendering any affiftance to General Prefcott, he took French leave, not forgetting to carry with him a cheft well lined, in order to render his refidence at Antigua comfortable.

pofe, the fort was no way better than when it fell into our hands, except being cleaner, and fupplied with provifions. On the 12th of October, a fchooner bearing a flag of truce, arrived from Victor Hughes; in it came Captain Eifton, of the 35th regiment,[y] for a fupply of money and baggage for our captured countrymen, with which he returned in two days to Point à Pitre. General Prefcott had taken the precaution to order all the batteries along the coaft, as well as thofe on the paffes of the Palmifte, to be deftroyed, their guns fpiked, and magazines blown up; but, owing to the fhortnefs of the time allowed for it, and the weaknefs of the force employed, the enemy foon got them repaired to ufe againft us. Captain Bowen, in the Terpfichore, was difpatched to Trois Riviere, to deftroy a battery there,[z] where he faw and fired on the enemy, who were marching in great force towards the heights of Falmifte. On which he returned, and informed the Admiral of this, by whom the intelligence was inftantly forwarded to General Prefcott, who had fent Captain Thomas of the 28th regiment (his aid-de-camp) to requeft fome feamen to reinforce his garrifon, which were moft readily granted by the Admiral. While Captain Thomas was on board the Boyne, the enemy, to his great aftonifhment, were feen on the heights of Palmifte. As there were a few royalifts about the General, fome

[y] The republican officer who came with him informed us that he faw the execution of the unfortunate royalifts, and that twenty-feven heads were ftruck off in feven minutes and a half!

[z] On the 19th of October the Admiral fent Lieutenant Skynner with a party of feamen to a battery at the N. W. end of the town, from whence he brought off fome cannon and mortars.

of whofe flaves were with the enemy, of courfe he ought to have received earlier information of their approach; but this fhews how all intelligence was withheld from us. For ten days after the General had withdrawn the whole of his force into the fort, he occafionally fent parties into the town, as the Boyne ftill kept the enemy quiet there; but in a fhort time they got fome guns up to an eminence, named by us the White-houfe Battery, that obliged the Admiral to weigh anchor: but he ftill continued to hover about the coaft, occafionally fending reinforcements and provifions, and keeping up a conftant intercourfe with General Prefcott in the fort. In the courfe of this bufinefs the Boyne was frequently engaged with the different batteries, and was expofed to great danger from the mortars, which the enemy began to play upon us with much judgment. On the 20th of October, the battery on Houelmont opened on the Terpfichore, but without effect. Our garrifon in the fort threw fome fhells which drove them from thence; they, however, foon returned again to their guns. The next day they again attacked the frigate, and hit her; which obliged Captain Bowen to get near the land, out of the direction of their guns. On the 23d, the White-houfe Battery, having feveral heavy guns mounted, began a fmart fire on the Boyne, which was returned from her lower deckers; afterwards we engaged a battery, into which the enemy had juft come, at the N. W. end of the town, from whence we drove them; but being obliged to haul off fhore occafionally, they at length completed their purpofe, but not fo as to be able to hinder us from approaching

the land to keep up an intercourfe with the garrifon. On this
fervice (as on every other) Captain Bowen eminently diftinguifhed
himfelf, having anchored the Terpfichore, within a fhort diftance
of the fort, in a bay under Houelmont. On the 25th the Quebec,
Captain Rogers, Beaulieu, Captain Riou, and Zebra, Captain
Vaughan, arrived from a cruife. The enemy now increafed their
forces daily in this part of the ifland, preffing into their fervice all
the negroes who were on the different eftates; and if from timi-
dity or any other caufe they demurred, they were inftantly fhot:
from the fhip we faw them firing on fome negroes of their own,
who, from fear, were endeavouring to get off. On the night of
the 26th, Lieutenant James, with a party of feamen, marched out
of the fort to the military hofpital, which he fet on fire, being a
place that the enemy would foon have made a confiderable poft
againft us. On the 29th, the Boyne, as ufual failing towards the
fort, was becalmed by the high land of Houelmont, and being
within a fhort diftance, was cannonaded from that battery for feveral hours. From the height of its fituation none of our guns could
be brought to bear againft it; however, after confiderable danger,
the fhip got out of the bay without any damage. On the 5th of
November, the enemy opened ten batteries againft the fort at the
fame inftant, and a party of them, with a field-piece, under cover
of the night, had taken poft on the brow of the hill under which
the Terpfichore and Experiment were anchored. As foon as the
feamen were arranged at day-break, to wafh the decks as ufual,
they were furprifed by a heavy fhower of mufketry from over their

heads. The Experiment endeavoured to get away, but being totally becalmed, it was fome time before fhe could accomplifh it. (Captain Miller had gone on board the Vanguard, and Captain Skynner was then in the Boyne, receiving his commiffion.[a]) Captain Bowen, with a prefence of mind that never forfook him, ordered up all the mufkets that could be procured, and, encouraging his men with great fpirit and fome effect, returned the fire of the enemy, who now brought their field-piece to bear on the fhip; he was therefore obliged to weigh anchor, and get out of the bay as well as he could, his great guns being totally ufelefs from the elevated fituation of the enemy: two or three only of our people were wounded, though the deck was ftudded with mufket-balls. The fort[b] was now clofely invefted by land; by the fea a communication was continued the whole fiege, Captain Bowen, in the Terpfichore, never relaxing for a moment in his exertions to ferve and affift the garrifon. The water in the tank being bad (the enemy having cut off the aqueduct that fupplied it), General Prefcott ordered an armed party every morning and evening to the river Galion, to protect thofe fent thither for water. This was

[a] On the 2d of November, Captain Miller was promoted to the command of the Vanguard, Captain Sawyer being removed to the Affurance, vice Captain Bryer, deceafed; and Lieutenant Launcelot Skynner of the Boyne, was appointed commander of the Experiment, vice Captain Miller.

[b] Fort Matilda, formerly Fort Charles, was at firft a battery only, erected to command the road; afterwards it was enclofed as a depot for arms and ammunition in cafe of infurrection among the flaves; and during the laft war the French added to its outworks, which were now totally in ruins, but ferved the enemy, particularly thofe on the oppofite fide of the Galion river, as trenches, and effectually covered their mufketry that commanded the principal works of the befieged: in fhort, the fort was completely commanded on the three fides by land, fo that not a man in it could move without being feen by the enemy.

continued during the whole fiege; cohorns and grape-fhot being fired into the ravines and woods beyond the river, and other precautions taken, thefe parties met with little moleftation. All the buildings in the fort being deftroyed by the fire of the enemy, the garrifon was obliged to take fhelter in the Bomb-proof, a clofe and unwholefome confinement in this climate. On the 6th of November, Victor Hughes fent an infolent fummons to General Prefcott, to furrender the fort in two hours, which if not complied with, no further terms would be offered, and the whole garrifon would be put to the fword. To this the General made a fhort anfwer, " that he would defend it as a foldier to the laft extremity." The inftant the hour was expired that the General allowed the French officer to return to Victor Hughes, he opened a heavy fire from all his batteries againft the republicans, and continued it through the day without any return from them. Some ftores and provifions were about this period fent to the garrifon from Dominica, and the merchants of St. Pierre alfo made a welcome prefent of refrefhments; the enemy at the fame time began to fupply their advanced batteries with neceffaries by fea in fmall boats, that, keeping clofe in fhore, evaded our cruifers, and landed at the town of Baffe Terre. On the 12th of November, the Boyne was expofed for fome time to a heavy fire from feveral batteries; one fhell burft immediately over her, but without doing any mifchief. At nine A. M. on the 14th of November, the Beaulieu, being then off Vieu Fort, made a fignal to the Admiral, of an enemy of fuperior force being in fight. Immediately all hands were ordered to quarters, and every preparation made to give them a warm reception; at length three line-of-battle ſhips hove in ſight, which, to our great joy, proved to be a rein-forcement from England; the Majeſtic, Captain Weſtcott, with Vice Admiral Caldwell's flag on board; the Theſeus, Captain Cal-der; and Bellona, Captain Wilſon: by them we were informed that Sir John Vaughan had arrived at St. Pierre, and Sir Charles Grey had given up the command to him. Sir John Jervis, worn down by long and ſevere exertions, the fatigues of which were augmented by his anxiety for the welfare of the ſervice, that not all his exertions could promote without the arrival of a ſtrong reinforcement, together with the unhealthineſs of the climate, found himſelf no longer able to continue on this ſtation, and there-fore, to the great grief of General Preſcott, was obliged to give up his command to Admiral Caldwell, and embarking his ſeamen (under Lieutenant James) from Fort Matilda, ſailed for St. Pierre; when, every thing being arranged and ſettled between the ſeveral commanders, Sir Charles Grey and his ſuite embarked once more with Sir John Jervis on board the Boyne; on the 27th of Novem-ber they ſailed for England, and after a tedious voyage (being for near a month toſſed about in the Channel by contrary winds) arrived at Spithead the 21ſt of January 1795.

As we left General Preſcott in a perilous ſituation, it may be proper to give an account of the concluſion of the ſiege, though

U

it comes not within the original plan of my work, which profeffed only to relate the events that took place under the immediate command of Sir Charles Grey and Sir John Jervis. This I am enabled to do from the communication of a brave and intelligent friend who was there during the whole fiege. On the 29th of November, Captain Cockburne, aid-de-camp of General Sir John Vaughan, was fent by his Excellency to Fort Matilda, with the unwelcome news that no more men could be fent thither. On the 5th of December, General Prefcott difpatched Captain Thomas, his aid-de-camp, to the Commander in Chief, with an account of the fort being almoft in ruins; this officer returned thither on the 7th, and found that the baftion towards the river Galion was totally filenced, and fo completely commanded by the enemy's mufketry, that not a man could approach it; the adjoining curtain was much in the fame ftate; the baftion towards the town was giving way, and expected to tumble into the ditch every moment. General Prefcott no longer thought of defence, but to fecure his fmall garrifon, now highly neceffary for the defence of the other iflands, the unparalleled mortality having left them almoft without troops. The peftilential fever had been, in proportion, more fatal to the officers than the men; in the garrifon, for inftance, there was no officer of intermediate rank between the General and his aid-de-camp Captain Thomas, who was fecond in command. On the 9th of December, this officer was difpatched to Admiral Thompfon, and after the plan of embarkation was fettled, he returned to the fort, and the evacuation com-

menced at nine o'clock on the 10th of December, and was conducted with fo much fkill, that not a man was loft. In the morning two of the garrifon deferted to the enemy; but the General
had concealed his intentions fo well, that not the leaft intelligence
of it feems to have been given by them. There was no interruption to the retreat except a few mufket-fhots on the beach, from
one of which that active officer Captain Bowen was badly wounded
in the face. The enemy, unconfcious of this movement, cannonaded and bombarded the fort as ufual, until two o'clock the
next morning, though the embarkation had been completed by
eleven the preceding night. The whole force that marched out
of Fort Matilda, was between four and five hundred : fome of
them were fent to the Ifle de Saintes and Antigua, and the remainder to Martinique. Thus concluded a fiege of eight weeks
and two days, during the whole of which General Prefcott evinced
the moft perfect coolnefs and true foldierly refolution,·neither ap-
palled by the tremendous and well-directed fire conftantly, both
night and day, kept up againft the fort, nor by the infolent and
threatening fummonfes of Victor Hughes.[c] In the handfomeft
manner he bore teftimony to the zeal and activity of Sir John
Jervis, who relaxed not in his attention to the wants of the garrifon, till he was obliged to quit the ftation; leaving however,
in Captain Bowen, a man whofe exiftence feemed to be preferved,
amidft the greateft dangers, for the fervice of his country. Admiral

During the fiege a cannon ball took off the fore part of the General's hat. He coolly obferved, "that a
mifs was as good as a mile!"

Thompſon had his ſhare of praiſe too for the manner in which he had conducted the embarkation. During the ſiege ſeventeen were killed, and ſeventy-nine were wounded. General Preſcott immediately repaired to Saint Pierre, at Martinique, where he received the well-earned thanks and congratulations of all ranks, for his ſpirited and gallant defence of Fort Matilda. Victor Hughes,[d] on taking poſſeſſion of the fort, ordered the monument that had been erected over General Dundas, to be deſtroyed, and his remains thrown into the river Galion; a conduct as mean and brutal, as it was undeſerved. I cannot conclude without mentioning the death of that gallant officer, Captain Faulknor, commanding the Blanche frigate of thirty-two guns, who, on the 5th of January, fell in with the republican frigate, La Pique of thirty-eight guns, off the harbour of Point à Pitre; the action was maintained with the

So much having been ſaid of this man, it may be agreeable to the reader to be informed of his origin, and purſuits in the former part of his life.—Victor Hughes was originally a petty inn-keeper at Baſſe Terre, Guadaloupe; from whence he was driven for ſome miſdemeanor, and became maſter of a ſmall trading veſſel at St. Domingo; then a lieutenant in the French navy; and afterwards a deputy in the national aſſembly: from whence he came out to the Weſt Indies as commiſſioner, with controlling powers over the commanders of the army and navy. His abilities were certainly good, his courage and perſeverance undoubted; but, from the ferocity of his character, he was both feared and hated. Colonel Drummond, who with his ſmall party was taken at Point Bacchus, relates that the republicans put to death all the ſick they found in the hoſpital at Petit Bourg, many of the women, and ſome children, cutting off heads, and otherwiſe mutilating the bodies; that, as the men who ſurrendered with him at Point Bacchus, fainted in their march, they were inſtantly bayonetted; the Colonel himſelf was, by particular directions from Victor Hughes, ordered to clean the priſon ſhip in turn with the others; but from this diſgrace he was relieved by the dutiful attachment of his men, who would not permit it: his food and lodging were the ſame as the reſt, no attention being paid to his rank; but from the reſpect and good behaviour of his men, not one of whom would deſert from him. A great number of people of all ages, ſexes, and conditions, were condemned to the guillotine by this inexorable tyrant, all of whom were conducted in boats round the priſon ſhip, in order to diſtreſs and intimidate the Britiſh priſoners.

greateft fury and obftinacy for five hours, during which Captain Faulknor fell by a mufket-ball as he was a fecond time lafhing the bowfprit of La Pique to the capftern of his own fhip. The lofs of this brave man muft be deplored by every friend to the fervice; his courage and determined bravery had been often tried, and always with fuccefs, as in the courfe of this work I have frequently had occafion to mention. On his death the command devolved on the firft lieutenant, Mr. Watkins, who continued the action in a manner that did him immortal honour. The French fhip having loft her main and mizen mafts, the Blanche took her in tow, ftill continuing the engagement, when the ftern ports not being large enough, they blew the upper tranfom beam away, and fired into her bows for three hours. The marines under Lieutenant Richardfon, kept fo well directed a fire, that not a man could appear on her forecaftle until fhe ftruck; fixty-feven of her crew were dead on the decks; many had been thrown overboard; one hundred and ten wounded were landed at the Saintes; and one hundred and feventy-four were taken to Marti-nique. The Blanche had ten killed, including the Captain, and twenty-four wounded. Captain Faulknor's exertions in forwarding the fervice on every occafion, both during, and fince the campaign, were unremitting. Indeed the Englifh caufe in the Weft Indies, at this inftant, could hardly have received a deeper wound than it did by the death of this brave and zealous man.

APPENDIX.

APPENDIX.

Head Quarters, Barbadoes, Wednesday, Jan. 22, 1794.

Parole, St. Domingo.   C. S. Williamson.

The Commander in Chief, having nearly finished all his arrangements to open the campaign with vigour, thinks it neceffary, during the few days the troops remain at Barbadoes, to give out the orders proper for the regulation and conduct of the troops; and he anxioufly calls upon every commanding officer of brigades, regiments, and corps, to fupport him in the due and ftrict obfervance thereof. The object of the campaign is to complete the conquest of the French West India Islands. Great fufficiency of provifions and a numerous train of artillery are provided. The General is fo thoroughly convinced of the zeal and intelligence of the officers and foldiers under his command, that he knows many orders upon the prefent occafion are unneceffary; yet, to fhorten orders in future, it may not be improper to explain to the foldiers the fatal confequences of ftraggling ever fo little away from camp

b

in queft of plunder; it is next to a certainty they will fall ignobly by the hands of the country people: or if they fhould efcape, they may depend upon fuffering the fevere punifhment due to difobeying military orders; as the General will never allow (while he has the honour to command fuch troops) practices of that nature to gain ground, as that alone, in time, will defeat the braveft army in the world, and render all their efforts ufelefs. The Britifh foldiers cannot be ignorant of the high reputation they have always acquired for obedience, attention, and expertnefs, in arms; and confequently they muft be fenfible how much their king and country expect from them: and the General is impreffed with every affurance, that the troops will not difappoint them upon this occafion. The General takes the liberty to affure them, that they are able to fight any troops upon earth; and he will be anfwerable that it would not be a conteft of ten minutes between this army and the beft troops of France, whether the affair was to be decided by fire or bayonet. This laft method is always to be preferred, but much more fo when acting againft fuch bad troops as the army we are now to be oppofed to, the enemy being made up chiefly of negroes and mulattoes, with a very fmall proportion of regular troops; to be beat by whom would be fo difgraceful, that he cannot entertain the moft diftant thought of it. The prefent diftracted ftate of France makes it impoffible to fupport them, therefore it only requires the ufual perfeverance and gallantry of Britifh foldiers to conquer the firft ifland that an attack is made upon, which will certainly decide the fate of the whole,

3

fhorten the campaign, and put an honourable end to the labour and exertion of the troops. The General thinks it a duty incumbent on him, and which he doubts not will be taken well, to point out further what he thinks neceffary, either for their own particular good, or that more noble object, the good of their king and country. The General defires the foldiers will confider what hardfhips muft attend their profeffion; that there is as much true honour in bearing them with manly fortitude, as in forcing the cannon of an enemy; patience under difficulties being one of the firft virtues in a military character, and without which no man, however brave, will ever be a foldier. In times like the prefent fome facrifice of convenience muft always be made to neceffity; at the fame time the foldiers may be affured that every attention will be paid by the Commander in Chief, and every other officer, to have them well fupplied with every article that the nature of the fervice will admit. On the other hand, he hopes the foldiers will be fo thoroughly convinced of this, that not one of them will be fo loft to honour and virtue, and the fervice of their country, as not readily and moft cheerfully to put up with every inconvenience, and even to the fcarcity of provifions, if it fhould fo happen. The General means to carry the bufinefs through with as little lofs as poffible, and with the ftricteft attention to the prefervation of the troops: to this end he expects that every duty required will be carried forward by the troops without the leaft unfoldier-like behaviour or complaint, and that all orders will be ftrictly obeyed. The army is fent to carry on honourable war

4

againſt the French colonies, and by their conduct, in preſerving the perſons and properties of the peaceable inhabitants, to conciliate the minds of the people to the Britiſh government; therefore the General determinately aſſures the troops, that he will allow of no drunkenneſs or licentious behaviour, no burning of churches, houſes, or edifices of any deſcription, without orders, or plundering in any ſhape whatever. All perſons that with their property remain in their habitations, ſhall be treated with humanity. No violence to be offered, particularly to women, on any pretence whatever. The ſtricteſt ſubordination and diſcipline to be preſerved throughout the whole army; and the commanding officer of brigades, regiments, and corps, muſt be reſponſible accordingly to the Commander in Chief.—The commanding officer will be careful that theſe orders, and every other that comes out, are diſtinctly read to their men by an officer, and be clearly underſtood by both officers and ſoldiers.—However it may hurt the General's feelings, he is determined to make immediate examples of all thoſe who ſhall preſume to diſobey his orders; more particularly that part of them relative to plundering, ill treatment of peaceable inhabitants, or firing of houſes, &c. And Captain Vipond, provoſt marſhal, has his orders to execute upon the ſpot every offender caught in ſuch horrid acts, without trial.—It may be neceſſary here to acquaint all officers' ſervants (not ſoldiers), and followers of the army of every deſcription, that they are ſubject to military law, and liable in like manner with the troops to the puniſhment of death, or corporal puniſhment, according to the nature of the offence. Each regiment and corps will apprize them of this, that ignorance may not be pleaded as an excuse. The success of this army totally depends upon a proper and strict degree of order and discipline being maintained; the General therefore again calls upon officers of every rank to assist him in enforcing it; for the whole are not to suffer by a disorderly few, who, if allowed to go on, would be the destruction of the whole army.

The provost marshal's guard to mount to-morrow morning at six o'clock, consisting of one sergeant, two corporals, twelve privates; and Captain Vipond will direct patroles to go out as he judges necessary, for the purpose of preserving order and regularity.—William Allen, sergeant major, of the forty-eighth regiment, is appointed deputy to the provost marshal; Captain Scott, of the sixth regiment, to act as major to that regiment; and Quarter Master William Haugh to do the duty of adjutant till further orders.—Carpenters are much wanted to expedite the equipment of hospital ships, and other necessary work on board the fleet; returns to be given in by each corps to-morrow of the number of carpenters they have, and such as they can furnish; to be supplied on the application of Captain Armstrong, assistant to the quarter master general, who will receive and take care to return them on board their respective transports. Working parties from the troops afloat are necessary for the same purpose, and will be supplied in rotation, by corps, with a proper proportion of non-commissioned officers, on the application of Captain Armstrong to the officers commanding regiments or battalions. The fixth regiment, and fuch of the flank companies not yet completed with camp equipage, will receive it on board the Sincerity brig to-morrow morning at fix o'clock. The quarter mafters of the refpective battalions will attend to receive it.—Lieutenant Geyer of the fixty-feventh regiment to do duty with the fixth regiment.—Provoft's guard, firft battalion grenadiers. One fergeant, nine privates of the ninth regiment on board the army brig to be landed this evening, and to march to St. Ann's, where they are to remain till further orders. The light companies at St. Ann's Caftle will fire ball this evening, &c. &c.

Lieut. Colonel Gomm was left to command at Barbadoes.

FURTHER ORDERS BEFORE EMBARKATION.

ORDERS. *Barbadoes, January* 24, 1794.

EXTRACT.

THE fafety of an army depending in a great meafure upon the guards and out-pofts, they cannot be too vigilant; therefore the Commander in Chief expects, that whatever poft or guard an officer is ordered to take, he will firft vifit his fituation and ground around it, and poft his centinels fo as to render it out of the power of the enemy to furprife him. It is the greateft difgrace that can poffibly befall an officer; and fo much fo in the General's opinion, that any officer, or non-commiffioned officer, who fhall fuffer himfelf to be furprifed, muft not expect to be forgiven.—— All out-pofts to fortify themfelves as well as they can, to prevent any infult from parties of the enemy. The troops always to form two deep; and, the roads being fo narrow in the ifland, it will be neceffary for them to march by files: if there is room to do other-wife, the commanding officer will be the beft judge.—The foldiers will bear in mind the ufe of the bayonet, which in poffeffion of, they can have no excufe for retreating for want of ammunition, the bayonet being the beft and moft effectual weapon in the hands of a gallant Britifh foldier; in which mode of attack (the General affures them) no troops upon earth are equal to them. In cafe of a night attack, ammunition and firing are totally out of the quef-tion, and the bayonet is ever to be preferred and made ufe of. Every reafon is in favour of this fyftem; amongft many others the following, viz. It conceals you and your numbers from the ene-my; the enemy direct their fire wherever they fee or hear fire, confequently fire upon each other, whilft you are concealed, and they fall an eafy prey. The General affures the troops of this from his own repeated experience; and the foldiers may rely in confi-dence upon him, that if it is ftrictly adhered to, it will feldom, if ever, fail of fuccefs.—As it may be neceffary at particular times to order the grenadiers, light infantry, and advanced corps, to retire, in order more effectually to fecure the defeat of the enemy, the Commander in Chief thinks it neceffary to apprize the army of this, to prevent any alarm fuch an appearance might otherwife occafion amongft the foldiers.—Weak and fickly men are not to embark with their regiments or corps; proper meafures will be taken to get thofe men to their regiments as foon as they are in a ftate fit for duty. No women to come on fhore till particularly ordered, &c.

The undernamed are the officers of Royal Engineers to ferve the army on the expedition.

Colonels . . . . Elias Durnford, Chief Engineer.
John Chillcotts.
Robert Douglas.
Captains . . . . William Johnfton.
James Gieddes.
Lewis Hay.
1ft Lieutenants Richard Downe.
Douglas Lawfon.
Richard Fletcher.
2d Lieutenant   Elias Walker Durnford.

No emigrants allowed to go as fervants or otherwife from Barbadoes with the expedition, without particular leave from the Commander in Chief; nor any negroes to be hired by the officers, without the confent of their owners.

9

Head Quarters, Riviere Sallée, Feb. 6, 1794.

GENERAL ORDERS.

Parole, MARTINICO.   C. S. MORNE.

Field Officer for the day, Lieut. Colonel Buckridge.

The army will halt to-day.

THE Commander in Chief cannot but exprefs the higheft fenfe he entertains of the exertion of the officers and foldiers in a long fatiguing march yefterday, and the orderly behaviour of the men during the whole march, and which muft at all times demand his utmoft attention; and he affures them the fame conduct will (and fpeedily) put an end to the campaign.—The Commander in Chief is pleafed to order an extra day of frefh provifions and rum to be iffued out to the men this day as foon as poffible.—The regiments which loaded yefterday on their march will draw their pieces immediately; and no regiment to load in future without orders, except the advanced guard.—A general court martial to be convened immediately for the trial of William Milton, of the Englifh light dragoons, and Samuel Price, of the black dragoons, for robbery; and all fuch prifoners as fhall be brought before them. Capt. Cunningham, and Jacques and Falice, to appear as witneffes.

c

Lieutenant Colonel Blundell, Prefident.

Lieutenant Colonel Johnfton.

Major Watfon.

Major Rofs.

Major Baillie.

Third battalion grenadiers . . . . . . 2 Captains.

Second light infantry . . . . 1 Ditto.

Third ditto . . . . 1 Ditto.

Third brigade . . . . 4 Ditto.

Names of the members, and dates of their commiffions, to be given in immediately to Major Lyon, deputy quarter mafter general, acting judge advocate. Lift of the evidence for and againft to be given in at the fame time. The quarter mafters of the different regiments at head quarters to give in to the quarter mafter general a return of the effective ftrength immediately.

AFTER ORDERS.   *Feb.* 7, 1794.

WILLIAM MILTON, private in the detachment of Britifh light dragoons, and Samuel Price, a negro, attached to the dragoons, tried by a general court martial, of which Lieutenant Colonel Bryan Blundell was prefident, for having entered the houfe of

Jacques, an inhabitant of this place, and robbing him of a fum of money, are both found guilty of the crime laid to their charge; and, by virtue of the power and authority vefted in the court by the fourth article of the twenty-third fection of the articles of war, the faid prifoners, William Milton and Samuel Price, are adjudged to fuffer death; which is approved of by the Commander in Chief, and the general court martial is diffolved.

The Commander in Chief feels moft fenfibly, and laments the neceffity of making examples fo immediately after landing, not-withftanding the ftrongeft and moft pointed orders given by him fo recently againft every kind of irregularity and improper beha-viour in foldiers on fervice, but particularly againft this very crime committed by the prifoners. Determined, however, to have his orders obeyed, to preferve difcipline in the army, which is fo effential to its fuccefs, and to prevent a repetition of crimes fo bafe, difgraceful, and deteftable, the prifoners, William Milton and Samuel Price, are ordered to be executed at eight o'clock to-morrow morning. The troops to parade at feven o'clock to-mor-row morning, in readinefs to attend the execution. The ninth and fifteenth regiments to fend four men each in augmentation of the caftle guard in the rear of the head quarters. Six mules will be delivered to each of the flank battalions, and four to each regi-ment, at nine o'clock to-morrow morning, at the quarter mafter general's.

12

Head Quarters, *Riviere Sallée, Feb.* 8, 1794.

Parole, WHYTE. C. S. BATTERIES.

Field Officer of the day, Major Watſon.

THE Commander in Chief hopes the awful ſcene of this morning
will have its proper effect, and not lay him again under the moſt
feeling and painful neceſſity of repeating it, but which muſt certainly be the unhappy caſe in the perſons of future offenders.
The General could not be juſtified in the eyes of his king and
country, and this army he has the honour to command, in acting
otherwiſe, their exiſtence and ſucceſs depending (of which every
good thinking ſoldier muſt be ſenſible) upon a proper degree of
diſcipline and ſubordination, with the moſt minute and ſtricteſt
obedience to orders, &c.

The General has the pleaſure to announce to the army the
complete ſucceſs of Brigadier General Whyte, at the head of the
third light infantry, in gallantly ſtorming and taking the batteries of
Cape Solomon and Bourgis. In Cape Solomon were four thirty-ſix
pounders and two twenty-four pounders; in Bourgis three twenty-
four pounders, all in perfect order to turn againſt the enemy; with
powder and ſhot in abundance. This ſucceſs opens a near communication with the fleet, by enabling them to come into Ance

d'Arlet Bay, with every fupply the army may be in want of; and what ftill renders it more valuable, carried with the lofs only of one man.

Head Quarters, Riviere Sallée, Feb. 9, 1794.

Parole, DUNDAS.   C. S. GROS MORNE.

Field Officer of the day, Major Baillie.

THE Commander in Chief has again the pleafure to announce to the troops the further fuccefs of his majefty's arms towards the conqueft of the ifland of Martinico, by the able conduct of Major General Dundas, and the gallantry and fpirit of the troops under his command, in attacking the enemy's troops under the command of Monf. Bellgarde at Trinité with bayonets, and putting them totally to the rout with great flaughter, he narrowly efcaping with a few followers into Fort Royal. The Major General with great fpirit followed up the blow, and took poffeffion of the very ftrong fort of the Gros Morne, where the Englifh colours are now flying.

He has alfo the pleafure to add the gallantry of the feventieth regiment, commanded by Lieutenant Colonel Johnfton, and led by Colonel Dundas, who with fo much fpirit and prompitude attacked the enemy pofted upon Morne Charlotte Pied, and put them totally to flight, taking poffeffion of that important commanding ground looking down upon Pigeon Ifland, which, when attacked (in conjunction with Brigadier General Whyte) and taken, will enable the Englifh fleet to come up into Fort Royal Harbour, in full view of the enemy's Forts of Bourbon and Royal.

The Commander in Chief is happy in the opportunity of making honourable mention of Captain Nares of the feventieth regiment, who led the advanced guard with fo much true courage and judgment in the above attack, as reported to him in the ftrongeft manner by Colonel Dundas.

Head Quarters, Riviere Sallée, Feb. 11, 1794.

Parole, GORDON.   C. S. CASE NAVIRE.

THE Commander in Chief is happy again to affure the army of the progrefs of our arms towards the reduction of Martinico. Colonel Sir Charles Gordon, and Captain Rogers commanding a fquadron of his Majefty's fhips, by their good conduct, activity, and fpirit, have made a landing good at Cafe Pilote, and taken all the batteries upon the coaft from Cape Pilote to Cafe Navirre. The gallantry of the troops, in charging and putting to flight the enemy wherever they dared to appear, was never more confpicuous.

Head Quarters, Riviere Sallée, Feb. 12, 1794.

Parole, WHYTE.   C. S. PIGEON ISLAND.

Field Officer of the day, Major Baillie.

IT is with the utmoſt ſatisfaction the Commander in Chief announces to the army the capture of Pigeon Iſland, which ſurrendered yeſterday morning about eleven o'clock, being a poſt of great ſtrength, and of the utmoſt importance towards the ſucceſs of our future operations. The Commander in Chief gives his thanks to Brigadier General Whyte, who commanded and conducted this ſervice with ſuch ſpirit and ability as to do him honour. Likewiſe to Colonel Symes, quarter maſter general, for his able aſſiſtance and zeal upon the occaſion.——The Commander in Chief returns his thanks to Lieutenant Colonel Cloſe, who commanded the third battalion of light infantry; and to Major Manningham, for his conſpicuous exertions. Likewiſe to Lieutenant Colonel Paterſon and Major Manly, who commanded the royal artillery, which was well and ably ſerved; and to Colonel Durnford of the engineers.

The Commander in Chief gives his thanks to all the officers and ſoldiers employed on that difficult and particular ſervice, whoſe courage and exertions (ſo eminently manifeſted) merit the greateſt praiſe.

The Commander in Chief alfo has to offer his warmeft acknowledgments and obligations to Lieutenants Rogers and Rutherford,
commanding the feamen, and to all the other officers and feamen
of his Majefty's navy; whofe perfeverance, able affiftance, and good
conduct, contributed much to the capture of the ifland.

_____

Head Quarters, Riviere Sallée, Feb. 13, 1794.

GENERAL ORDERS.

Parole, YORK.   C. S. GLOUCESTER.

THE Commander in Chief is happy in the opportunity of expreffing the pleafure he received from the report of Major Lyon, deputy adjutant general, of the fpirited conduct of the fifteenth
regiment, commanded by Captain Pomier, in the attack of a very
ftrong poft of the enemy at eleven o'clock laft night, in which attack two hundred of the enemy were furprifed, and totally routed,
with fome lofs, and all their cattle, provifions, arms, &c. and fome
prifoners taken, with the lofs of one man only of the fifteenth
regiment killed, and two wounded.

The fifteenth regiment, at the fame time that they accept the
Commander in Chief's acknowledgments for their fpirited con-

duct, will allow him to fay, that if they had not fired, the furprife might have been more complete; and firing, he trufts, they will in future, in all night attacks, on all occafions, avoid, and which, they well know, how very ftrongly he recommended previous to the opening of the campaign; and he defires the commanding officers will turn back to their orders, and read them to the officers and men.

The Commander in Chief defires that the warm fenfe he entertains of the fpirited fervice of Captain de Rivigne (who commanded the howitzers in the fiege and capture of Pigeon Ifland, as reported by Brigadier General Whyte) may be made known to the army, &c.

Head Quarters, Heights of Brunot, Feb. 17, 1794.

Parole, CONQUEST.   C. S. ST. PIERRE.

Field Officer, Major Campbell.

THE Commander in Chief hopes that every care is taken of, and humanity fhewn to, the negroes attached to the regiments, and to all thofe employed with the army; and that they are victualled, attended to, and encouraged. This the commanding officers of regiments and corps, and every officer in all. departments, will

d

attend to, and inquire into: as many have fled from the camp, which muſt be owing to their having been neglected, or ill uſed by ſome of the men, ſuch treatment muſt be prevented in future, otherwiſe the army will ſuffer every inconvenience.

———————————

Head Quarters, Brunot, Feb. 19, 1794.

Parole, ST. PIERRE.   C. S. DUNDAS.

Field Officer, Colonel Coote.

THE Commander in Chief has the pleaſure to announce to the army the complete capture of St. Pierre, the moſt confiderable town in this iſland, which contains the greateſt part of its wealth, its roads crowded with ſhips and merchandiſe, now the prizes of the army and navy.

The Commander in Chief holds himſelf highly obliged to the troops for their ſpirited and cool conduct in the courſe of the attack yeſterday; and congratulates them upon ſo eaſy an acquiſition of the ſtrong ground hitherto occupied by the enemy, owing to the prompt and ſpirited movement of Lieutenant Colonel Buckridge, and the ſupport of the light infantry under Lieutenant Colonel Coote and Lieutenant Colonel Blundell: this being the very ground intended to be occupied, and eſſential for the impending ſiege. The ſixth, ninth, and ſecond light infantry, with all the artillery of the camp at Brunot, to march and form the line of the new camp at Sourier at day-break. The ſeventieth and fifteenth regiments to remain at the port of Matilda, and the covering of the landing place, till further orders.

The commiſſary to order the proviſions, &c. of the army to be eſcorted to the moſt convenient and contiguous ſituation for the ſupply of the army in their new poſition; which, from their preſent landing place, will be nearer than their former encampment. The cavalry, provoſt's, and every other department attendant on the army, to move to-morrow morning. The poſt of Colomb, occupied by Lieutenant Colonel Coote, to be retained by two companies, and that of Lieutenant Colonel Buckridge by one company.

No bullocks for draught, which are neceſſary for agriculture to the inhabitants, or milch cows, to be ſlaughtered by the army.

Head Quarters, Heights of Sourier, Feb. 22, 1794.

Parole, NAVY.   C. S. ANIMATION.

Field Officer, Major Campbell.

THE Commander in Chief faw with pleafure and furprife this morning the great progrefs that has been made in forming an excellent road for the battering train through fo difficult a country, and the fair profpect of the artillery fhortly arriving at the deftined ground. Nothing can exceed the order and indefatigability of the Britifh failors, and the zeal and pleafure with which they appear animated in the moft laborious exertions; he has remarked this with the utmoft fatisfaction.

He begs Captains Hervey, Kelly, and Carpenter, with the officers and men under their command, will accept his beft thanks and acknowledgments of how much he owes them. When the two fervices thus combine and co-operate, the greateft obftacles may be furmounted, and every difficulty vanifh. The Commander in Chief has given orders to the commiffary that the feamen fhall be amply fupplied with provifions and rum.

Head Quarters, Camp at Sourier, Feb. 24, 1794.

Parole, GREAT GUN.   C. S. MORTAR.

NOT that the Commander in Chief has any reafon whatever to fufpect the advanced pofts and guard of the camp are not alert, but, on the contrary, their fteadinefs and attention give him true fatisfaction: neverthelefs he thinks it right to warn them, that the enemy, in their prefent hopelefs fituation, may be defperate, and attempt to infult fome of the pofts: more they cannot do; but the flighteft advantage gained, their expiring caufe may for a moment be fpirited up to hold out a little longer, and caufe the lofs of a few brave men; this the Commander in Chief wifhes to avoid, and to make the conqueft of this valuable ifland of Martinico with the leaft lofs poffible, he being ever attentive and watchful of their prefervation. He particularly defires the advanced pofts will, if poffible, increafe their vigilance, and in cafe of an infult, to meet it coolly, not rifking themfelves by darting forward (this not being the time for fuch exertion), but to check their ardour, and content themfelves by ftanding on the defenfive, and repulfing the enemy, covering fteadily the bringing up the battering train to their deftined ground, which will very foon be completed, and the batteries ready to open powerfully upon the enemy from three points at one and the fame time; which done, the Commander in Chief affures the army that he has every reafon to believe they will be in poffeffion of the enemy's laft ftake in a little time, and honourably put an end to their labours.

The Commander in Chief again repeats his orders for all the out-pofts that are the leaft expofed to the enemy's fire, to fortify and fhelter themfelves, throwing up blinds at certain diftances to run behind when a fhell falls, and which will effectually fecure them.—In the trench of Lieutenant Colonel Coote's poft three or four crofs blinds fhould be made; and the engineer is immediately to order it. The advanced guns alfo to be guarded, to prevent a fhot damaging a wheel or carriage; which Lieutenant Colonel Paterfon will order to be done.

Head Quarters, Camp, Heights of Sourier, Feb. 28, 1794.

Parole, Push.   C. S. Forward.

Field Officer, Lieutenant Colonel Craddock.

Alexander Ross, fecond gunner, royal artillery, and Edward Brookes, of the royal Irifh artillery, tried by the general court martial, of which Lieutenant Colonel Buckridge was prefident, for abfenting themfelves five hours from the poft of Gros Morne; and on fufpicion of having robbed Madame Lamalle of a gold watch and chain, with various other articles, viz. fix filver fpoons, fix forks, and a large foup fpoon. The prifoners are further accufed of robbing a wafherwoman of fome wearing apparel belonging to Adjutant Wilkinfon, of the fixty-fourth regiment. The court, having maturely confidered the evidence in fupport of the charge againft the prifoners, together with what they had to advance in their defence, acquit the prifoners, Alexander Rofs, fecond gunner of royal artillery, and Edward Brookes, of the royal Irifh artillery, of the charge againft them of having robbed Madame Lamalle and the wafherwoman: but the prifoners, Alexander Rofs, of the royal artillery, and Edward Brookes, of the royal Irifh artillery, are both found guilty of abfenting themfelves from the poft of Gros Morne without leave, in breach of the fourteenth fection of articles of war, and are therefore adjudged to receive four hundred lafhes each on their bare backs.—The Commander in Chief approves of the above fentence, and directs, that the punifhment of four hundred lafhes each be inflicted on the prifoners to-morrow morning at feven o'clock, at the head of the Englifh and royal Irifh artillery.—The Commander in Chief is clearly of opinion that the prifoners, Alexander Rofs and Edward Brookes, were alfo guilty of the charge of robbery advanced againft them; but the evidence not being of that force to juftify the court martial in finding them guilty, they are fortunate in efcaping, and he thinks it will make a lafting impreffion on their minds; for the Commander in Chief affures them, had they been found guilty (however painful to him), they fhould have fuffered the laft punifhment, death, at the head of the army.

The prifoner Phelps, foldier in the fortieth regiment of foot, tried by the fame general court martial for defertion, is found guilty, in breach of the firft article of the fixth fection of the articles of war, and fentenced to receive eight hundred lafhes on his bare back, in the ufual manner. The Commander in Chief approves of the above fentence; but, in confideration of the great length of time the prifoner, John Phelps, has been confined, he is pleafed to pardon him; and hopes this inftance of lenity will make a deep and lafting impreffion on his mind, and induce him to behave like a good and faithful Britifh foldier to his king and country in future.

―――――――――――

Head Quarters, Camp, Sourier, March 5, 1794.

Parole, Aim.   C. S. Well.

EXTRACTS.

His Royal Highnefs Prince Edward, major general, to take the command of his Majefty's troops forming the inveftment of Fort Bourbon, on the Cafe Navire fide, and the camp at La Cofte, with all the pofts depending.

The Commander in Chief obferves the foldiers do not dig a trench round their tents to carry off the wet: the commanding officers of regiments and corps to order it to be done immediately, and to fend for the hammocks belonging to the round tents, to make the men as comfortable as poffible.

Captain J. A. Wetheral, and Lieutenant J. Vefey, of the eleventh foot, are appointed aid de camps to his Royal Highnefs Prince Edward, major general, and to be obeyed as fuch.—The Commander in Chief has the pleafure to announce, that a detachment of the fifteenth regiment, commanded by Lord Sinclair, and a detachment of light dragoons, commanded by Lieutenant Shadwell, and conducted by Captain Cunningham (his aid de camp), furprifed at ten o'clock this morning a ftrong corps of the enemy near Francois, which they had fet on fire. The enemy were completely furprifed, who had been burning, plundering, and murdering, wherever they went; thirty-fix were killed, with their chief, who was cut down by a light dragoon. Four prifoners were taken, who were hung up as an example to fuch rafcals in future; which method the General is determined uniformly to purfue with all fuch taken in arms.—The Commander in Chief returns his beft thanks to Lord Sinclair, Captain Cunningham, and Lieutenant Shadwell, for their zeal and exertion on this occafion; and to all the officers and men employed. The fire of Francois was extinguifhed, and only four houfes burnt. Our lofs only two men wounded.

Head Quarters, Camp at Sourier, March 9, 1794.

Parole, ADVANCE.   C. S. NEARER.

Field Officer, Major Baillie.

LIEUTENANT General Prefcot will advance, and poft the feventieth regiment to cover the new batteries; which done, the captain and fixty men, and fubaltern and thirty, pofted at and near
M. Ragout's houfe, to be withdrawn, excepting a ferjeant and
twelve men pofted on the height in the rear of that poft, which
muft be continued until further orders.   Surgeon's mate William
Wood, of the feventieth regiment, is appointed furgeon's mate
to the general hofpital in the Weft Indies.   The following gentlemen are appointed to act as affiftant engineers: Mr. Thomas
Hall, Lieutenant Fenton, forty-third regiment, Enfign Snell, fifteenth regiment, Enfign Garroway, king's Carolina regiment, and
M. la Granche.

========

Head Quarters, Camp at Sourier, before Fort Bourbon,
March 18, 1794.

THE gallant attack of the feamen, headed by Lieutenant Bowen
of the Boyne, in boarding the Gabarre, in the carinage of Fort

Royal, in open boats, at noon day yefterday, under a fhower of grape fhot and mufquetry from the garrifon, taking the captain, lieutenant, and twelve men prifoners, being all there were on board, and even firing fome of the guns of the Gabarre againft the fort, merits the higheft praife and admiration. This gallant tranf-action the Commander in Chief was a witnefs of, and takes this opportunity of repeating how perfectly fenfible he is of their me-ritorious fervices, with thofe of the navy in general, and of their unwearied exertion in forwarding his majefty's fervice in every way, and on this critical occafion; and begs they will accept of his beft thanks. Lieutenant Robertfon to do duty as major of brigade, in the room of M. B. Forbes, till further orders.

Head Quarters, Camp at Sourier, before Fort Bourbon, Friday, March 21, 1794.

Parole, FORT.   C. S. ROYAL.

Field Officer, Major Baillie.

DURING the prefent truce no relaxation of duty, vigilance, or preparation for a continuance of the fiege, to take place; on the contrary, every exertion to be ufed for opening again with more vigour than ever, fhould the prefent conference break of, by not agreeing on terms; which may be the cafe.

The Commander in Chief has great fatisfaction in congratulating the army on the moft important capture of Fort Royal, effected with fo much good conduct and gallantry, which he trufts muft lead to a fpeedy furrender of Fort Bourbon.—The firft battalion of grenadiers, commanded by Lieutenant Colonel Stewart, and third battalion of light infantry, commanded by Lieutenant Colonel Clofe, from camp la Cofte, with the third battalion of grenadiers, commanded by Lieutenant Colonel Buckridge, and firft light infantry, commanded by Lieutenant Colonel Coote, from the camp of Sourier, behaved with their ufual fpirit on the occafion, and fuch as muft always command fuccefs. Captain de Rivigne, of the royal artillery, has done his duty in fo excellent a manner, fhewing fuperior judgment in conducting the fire of the field pieces on the left, and fo effectually covering the approach of the troops, as has done him the greateft honour, and proves him to be a moft valuable officer.

The Commander in Chief acknowledges great obligations to the navy, on their gallant efcalade of Fort Royal, under the able conduct of Commodore Thompfon, with the affiftance of the Afia, Captain Brown; but particularly to Captain Faulkner of the Zebra, whofe gallantry and judgment have juftly gained him the admiration of the whole army.—Commodore Thompfon's judicious arrangement of the gun-boats and flat-boats, with the affiftance of Captain Rogers, who landed and entered the town of Fort

Royal from the fide of Tortenfon, contributed moft effentially to the fuccefs of the enterprife, in which the zealous affiftance and activity of Captain Sancée of the Guides, was highly meritorious and ufeful. The Commander in Chief's thanks are juftly due to every perfon employed on that fervice, which he gives with infinite pleafure and fatisfaction.

Head Quarters, Fort Royal, March 25, 1794.

Parole, FORT GEORGE.   C. S. FORT EDWARD.

Field Officer, Colonel Coote.

THE Commander in Chief orders Fort Bourbon now to bear the name of Fort George, and Fort Louis to bear the name of Fort Edward; and to be called fo in future.—The Commander in Chief, with heartfelt fatisfaction, congratulates the army on the complete conqueft of the ifland of Martinico, a moft important acquifition to his majefty's crown. He begs permiffion to return the army in general his warmeft thanks for their zeal, perfeverance, gallantry, and fpirit, fo eminently diftinguifhed, and never before exceeded, by every rank, from the general to the foldier, throughout this fervice; and this juftice he cannot fail to do them in the ftrongeft language to his majefty.—The works of the trenches to be levelled, and every preparation made by all departments for embarkation on another expedition. The tranfports are ordered round to Fort Royal; and the cannon, ordnance ftores, and every thing belonging to the engineer and military departments, to be conveyed down, ready to be embarked on board their refpective fhips, regularly, and with fuch method, that no fort of confufion or retardment may happen upon a fecond difembarkation. The artillery will always be the firft called for.—All officers of the army and navy to have permiffion to go into Fort George.

GENERAL ORDERS.

Head Quarters, Boyne, off Guadaloupe, June 4, 1794.

COLONEL Richard Symes is appointed brigadier general from the 25th of May, 1794, in the Weft Indies; and alfo governor of Guadaloupe, until his majefty's pleafure is known.

GENERAL ORDERS.   *Guadaloupe, June 8, 1794.*

COLONEL Francis Dundas is appointed Brigadier General from the 26th of May, 1794, in the Weft Indies. Surgeon Thomas

Wright, from the garrifon of Guadaloupe, to be purveyor of the general hofpital, vice Dundon, deceafed. The Honourable Captain Stewart, of the twenty-fecond regiment, to be extra aid de camp to the Commander in Chief.

GENERAL ORDERS.   *Guadaloupe, June* 10, 1794.

CAPTAIN Donkin, of the forty-fourth regiment, to do duty as major of brigade.

GENERAL ORDERS.   *Boyne, off Pointe a Pitre, June* 13, 1794.

THE Commander in Chief feels great fatisfaction in acquainting the army with his majefty's entire approbation of their gallant exertions and bravery during this campaign, to the time of the capture of Fort Bourbon (now Fort George), and the complete conqueft of the ifland of Martinique; which is communicated to him in a letter from the fecretary of ftate, bearing date the 22d of April, 1794, of which the following is an extract. " I am therefore to fignify " to you his majefty's moft perfect and entire approbation of your " conduct, and of the gallant behaviour of all the officers and fol- " diers under your command; and to defire that you will convey

" to them the juft fenfe his majefty entertains of the honour they
" have done themfelves, and of the fervices which they have ren-
" dered to their country."—The Commander in Chief has alfo
the pleafure of notifying to the army, that having made application for exempting it from paying poftage, his majefty has been
gracioufly pleafed to comply therewith; which is communicated
to him in a letter from the fecretary of ftate of the fame date, the
following being an extract. " His majefty is moft gracioufly
" pleafed to comply with your requeft that the army under your
" command whilft on fervice may be exempted from paying poft-
" age for their letters; and I fhall immediately fignify the fame to
" the poft mafter general."

GENERAL ORDERS. *Boyne, off Pointe a Pitre, June* 14, 1794.

Parole, LIGHT INFANTRY. C. S. ....

THE Commander in Chief thanks Brigadier General Dundas, and
the firft light infantry, under the command of Major Rofs, fupported by the thirty-ninth regiment, under Major Magan, for the
ufual fpirit with which they attacked the French camp at Point
Gabbare, and congratulates them on the complete fuccefs of it.—
The able and gallant conduct of Major Rofs, in leading the light

infantry fo handfomely to the charge, as reported by Brigadier General Dundas, demands the Commander in Chief's particular acknowledgments; and which he will not fail to report to the miniftry, to lay before his majefty.

GENERAL ORDERS.

Boyne, off Pointe a Pitre, Guadaloupe, June 15, 1794.

Parole, BOYNE.   C. S. ....

THE grenadier companies of the fixth, ninth, fifteenth, twenty-firft, fifty-fixth, fifty-eighth, fixtieth, fourth battalion of the fixty-fourth, fixty-fifth, and three companies from the Irifh regiments, to be formed into a battalion under the command of Lieutenant Colonel Fifher, of the fixtieth regiment. The light companies of the fixth, ninth, fifteenth, twenty-firft, fifty-fixth, fifty-eighth, fixtieth, fourth battalion of the fixty-fourth, fixty-fifth, and three companies from the Irifh regiments, to be formed into a battalion under the command of Lieutenant Colonel Gomm.

General Orders.   *Boyne, off Pointe a Pitre, June* 18, 1794.

Parole, ...   C. S. ....

THE Commander in Chief feels with great concern the neceſſity of again aſſembling part of the troops to diſlodge an enemy who have ſtolen into Pointe a Pitre, and the poſts in its neighbourhood, at the moment when the gallant General Dundas was expiring. He had hoped that the troops, whoſe meritorious ſervices had acquired ſo much glory during a moſt ſuccefsful campaign, would have found reſt and comfort during the remainder of this year at leaſt. Relying however on the cheerful and utmoſt exertions of the gallant troops he has the happineſs to command, he cannot entertain a doubt of finiſhing the ſervice ſpeedily and glorioufly, to enable the troops to return very ſoon to the quarters from whence they are now called forth to ſervice.

The Commander in Chief aſſures the troops that their ſituation on this extra ſervice ſhall be made as comfortable and agreeable to them as it is in his power to render it; and that no time ſhall be loſt in advancing againſt the enemy, confiſtent with the attention he always pays to the preſervation of his ſoldiers, not wantonly or prematurely expoſing them to danger.

The ſame conduct, good behaviour, and cool bravery, which gained ſuch rapid and complete ſuccefs hitherto, will inſure it on the preſent occaſion, againſt about five hundred regular troops, joined by a defpicable and motley crew of mulattoes and negroes, with fome feamen, the whole a forlorn hope, who put in here for the want of provifions, and at a time the forty-third regiment was weakened by ficknefs.

The troops to be ready to get into the flat boats to-morrow morning at three o'clock. The boats, when the men are embarked, are to affemble aftern of the Affurance forty-four gun fhip, there waiting for orders to proceed on fhore. The troops to carry on fhore with them three days provifions dreffed, one day's grog, and rum in kegs for another day: alfo to land with their tent blankets, camp kettles, water kegs, canteens, and hand hatchets; the failors to land with ditto and tomahawks.

The light infantry to be firft to land with two amuzettes, fupported by the battalion of grenadiers with two three-pounders.

The fixty-fifth regiment then to land with two fix-pounders; Captain de Rivignes commanding the artillery. After the troops are landed, and have got the heights oppofite, the fpare artillery, howitzers, ftores, &c. are to be landed at Grozier. The commanding engineer will land at the fame time all the artificers, and every thing belonging to his department, that no time whatfoever may be loft in forwarding the enterprife. The firft troops that land will immediately take advantage of the ftrongeft ground, houfes, &c. there pofting themfelves; not advancing until the whole are landed. Brigadier General Symes will direct the landing, and is to command the troops on fhore. The Commander in Chief has been pleafed to appoint Captain John Cunnyngham, of the forty-third regiment, to be deputy adjutant general, vice Lyon, deceafed.

GENERAL ORDERS. *Head Quarters, Grozier, Guadaloupe, June 20, 1794.*

THE Commander in Chief is much furprifed to find, from the report of Brigadier General Symes, that the feamen and foldiers ftraggle from camp in fearch of water, which, when found in the neighbourhood, is not fit for drinking, though it may anfwer for cooking. The Commander in Chief forbids any officer from quitting the poft of his company, except on duty; and directs that the rolls be called every two hours. If any foldier or feaman be found marauding or ftraggling from camp, he will be punifhed in the moft fevere manner. The officers commanding corps to fee their battalions fall in, and the rolls called, from which no officer is to be abfent, as the enemy are lurking about the pofts.

The piquets are not to fuffer any perfon to pafs them, without a pafs in writing from the brigadier general.

Each corps will fend an officer for orders to head quarters every day at ten o'clock, and an orderly ferjeant from each corps to attend conftantly. All applications for provifions to be made to Mr. Johnftone, the quarter mafter of the fixtieth regiment. Thefe orders, as well as all others, to be read to the men by an officer of each company. Captain Robins, of the fixtieth re-giment, to do duty with the fixty-fifth regiment; and Lieutenant Milnes, of the forty-ninth, with the ninth light infantry.

The Honourable Captain Stewart, of the twenty-fecond re-giment, having offered his fervices to the Commander in Chief on this prefent occafion, they are accepted; and he is ordered to do duty with the ninth grenadier company.

———————

GENERAL ORDERS. *Head Quarters, Grozier Camp, June* 21, 1794.

Parole, ENGLAND. C. S. PROSPERITY.

ON account of the brilliant fuccefs of his majefty's arms, and his allies, in France, by the complete victory gained by the Duke of York at the head of the Britifh, and alfo by the Auftrians, on the 26th of April laft, in which the French General Chapuey was made prifoner, with fifty-feven pieces of their cannon taken, and a great flaughter of their troops, with a very inconfiderable lofs of the Britifh troops and their allies, the Commander in Chief orders a *feu de joie* on the occafion at fix o'clock this evening; for which purpofe all the troops will be under arms and affemble with the na-val battalion at five o'clock, and are to be marched to a confpicuous fituation, in view of the enemy, to give three rounds of running fire. The whole of our artillery, drawn up in front of the line, are to fire three rounds. Each round of artillery to precede a round of fmall arms: running fire beginning at the right of the line; and to conclude with three hearty cheers.—Brigadier General Symes, who commands the line, will be fo good as to place and arrange the troops on this occafion, pointing out the ground they are to affemble upon. The whole navy will fire a *feu de joie*, and the troops under the command of Brigadier General Dundas at the camp at Berville, at the fame time.

The Commander in Chief defires that his long, fpirited, and determined orders, given out when the army failed from Barbadoes on the expedition to Martinico, dated the 22d of January, may be read to the troops, particularly to the feamen, many of whom have not ferved on fhore. This the commanding officers of corps and naval battalions will be anfwerable to the Commander in Chief is done; and at the fame time to affure their men, that however it may hurt his feelings, he will put the faid orders in full force upon any and every offender in future; for without ftrict difcipline and good order, no good fervice can poffibly be effected: and he again calls upon every officer in the army to affift him in this neceffary work. The troops to receive one day's frefh meat, and two days falt provifion and rum, to-morrow morning at day-break. Returns to be fent to the commiffary general this evening.

AFTER ORDERS.

CATTLE of every defcription to be brought to head quarters, or delivered to perfons ordered to receive them; and no perfon whatever to kill any beaft without orders. It is ftrictly forbid that any officer, foldier, or feaman, fhall prefume to take any negroes, except thofe delivered to them by the quarter mafter general's department. The marauding which has taken place obliges the General to remind the commanding officers of corps to refer to orders already given out on that head. It will give him extreme concern to be obliged to punifh with feverity fuch crimes; but as the exiftence of the army depends on its difcipline, it muft be maintained. The firft man caught in the act of plundering, to be hung on the fpot. The provoft is ordered to vifit the environs of the encampment, and to execute this order with the utmoft vigilance. Piquet to parade at fix in the evening.

Head Quarters, Grozier, June 24, 1794.

Parole, CAMBRAY.   C. S. YORK.

Field Officer for the day, Major Crofbie.

THE two divifions of marines are to do duty with the battalion of grenadiers under the command of Lieutenant Colonel Fifher.

The troops will be particularly careful of their camp kettles, canteens, and haverfacks, as no more can be procured for them.

Only two quarts of water per man can be iffued for the troops, and that early in the morning, from the men of war. Four days provifion to be iffued to the troops to-morrow morning.

━━━━━━━━

GENERAL ORDERS. *July* 6, 1794.

THE Commander in Chief has juft received another letter from the fecretary of ftate on the fubject of poftage of letters to this army, of which the following is a copy.

" SIR, *Whitehall, May* 8, 1794.

" As I find the poft mafter general is reftrained by law " from difcharging any letters from the payment of poftage, I " have, in order that the officers and foldiers under your com- " mand may receive their letters free of expence, notified to the " different army agents, that all letters for the faid officers and " foldiers, if fent to this office, will be forwarded to them. I " have accordingly directed that fuch letters fhall be put in a fe- " parate packet or bag, and addreffed to yourfelf, and tranfmitted " by each mail.

(Signed) " HENRY DUNDAS."

Extract from another Letter from Mr. Dundas *to Sir* Charles Grey, *K. B. May* 21, 1794.

" It is peculiarly grateful to his Majefty in directing me to
" fignify to you his moft entire and perfect approbation of your
" conduct, and of the gallant behaviour of all the officers and
" foldiers who ferved upon this occafion; and which you will con-
" vey to them in the moft particular manner, and that fuch impor-
" tant conquefts have been attained with fo little lofs on the part
" of his majefty. I take this opportunity of inclofing you the
" votes of thanks to you and Sir John Jervis, which I moved
" yefterday, with the unanimous concurrence of the Houfe. You
" will obferve they are to be officially communicated to you by the
" fpeaker. Similar votes were unanimoufly paffed by the Lords."

Extracts from the Votes of the Houfe of Commons.

" Refolved, nemine contradicente, That the thanks of this
" Houfe be given to Sir Charles Grey, Knight of the moft ho-
" nourable order of the Bath, for his late able, gallant, and me-
" ritorious conduct in the Weft Indies."
" Refolved, nemine contradicente, That the thanks of this
" Houfe be given to Lieutenant General Prefcott, his Royal High-
" nefs Major General Prince Edward, and Major General Thomas
" Dundas, and to the feveral officers of the army under the com-

" mand of Sir Charles Grey, for their late gallant conduct and
" meritorious exertions in the Weſt Indies."

" Reſolved, nem. con. That this Houſe doth highly approve
" and acknowledge the ſervices of the non-commiſſioned officers
" and private ſoldiers in the army ſerving under Sir Charles Grey
" in the Weſt Indies; and that the ſame be ſignified to them by
" the commanders of the ſeveral corps, who are deſired to thank
" them for their gallant behaviour."

" Ordered, That the ſpeaker do ſignify the ſaid reſolutions to
" Sir Charles Grey and Sir John Jervis."

Colonel Colin Graham, of the twenty-firſt regiment, is appointed brigadier general from the 26th of May, 1794.

Head Quarters, Martinique, July 13, 1794.

Parole, NORTHAMPTON.   C. S. BURFIELD.

A General court martial to aſſemble at St. Pierre's, Martinico, on
Friday next, the 25th inſtant, at eight o'clock, for the trial of
Brigadier General Sir Charles Gordon, lieutenant colonel of the
forty-firſt regiment of foot, and ſuch other matters as ſhall be

brought before them. The witneffes, both on the part of the prifoner and profecution, to attend; lifts whereof to be fent to Major of Brigade Lorraine, at St. Pierre's, immediately. The above general court martial to confift as follows.

Lieutenant General Prefcott, prefident.

And fuch other members as fhall be hereafter ordered.

———————————————

Boyne, off Pointe a Pitre, July 20, 1794.

Parole, BRITAIN.   C. S. ......

THE Commander in Chief orders a *feu de joie* to be fired this evening at fix o'clock, to celebrate the moft fignal victory that ever was gained over the French fleet, on the 1ft of June laft, by Earl Howe, in the Englifh channel. The French fleet confifted of twenty-fix fhips of the line, the Englifh fleet of twenty-five. Of the French feven fail of fhips of the line were taken, one funk, and many of them difmafted and crippled; fo that moft probably many more would fall into the hands of the Englifh. In fhort, the General has the fatisfaction to announce to the army the total ruin of the French fleet.

Head Quarters, St. Pierre, July 28, 1794.

Parole, JERVIS.   C. S. ....

THE Right Honourable Lord Loughborough having tranſmitted to the Commander in Chief the votes of thanks paſſed by the Houſe of Lords to himſelf, Lieutenant General Preſcott, his Royal Highneſs Prince Edward, and Major General Thomas Dundas, and all the other officers of this army; the Commander in Chief loſes no time in giving out the following copies of thoſe votes in general orders.

"*Die Mercurii.*

" Ordered, nemine diſſentiente, by the Lords ſpiritual and
" temporal, in parliament aſſembled, That the thanks of this
" Houſe be given to Sir Charles Grey, Knight of the moſt ho-
" nourable order of the Bath, for his late able, gallant, and me-
" ritorious conduct in the Weſt Indies."
              Signed,   G. ROSE, Clerk of Parliament.

"*Die Mercurii.*

" Ordered, nemine diſſentiente, by the Lords ſpiritual and
" temporal, in parliament aſſembled, That the thanks of this
" Houſe be given to Lieutenant General Preſcott, his Royal High-
" neſs Prince Edward, Major General Thomas Dundas, and to
" the ſeveral officers of the army under the command of Sir

" Charles Grey, for their late able, gallant, and meritorious con-
" duct in the Weft Indies."

Signed,   G. Rose, Clerk of Parliament.

May 21, 1794.

" Ordered, nemine diffentiente, by the Lords fpiritual and
" temporal, in parliament affembled, That this Houfe doth highly
" approve and acknowledge the fervices of the non-commiffioned
" officers and private men in the army ferving under Sir Charles
" Grey in the Weft Indies; and that the fame be fignified to them
" by the commanding officers of the feveral corps, who are de-
" fired to thank them for their gallant behaviour."

Signed,   G. Rose, Clerk of Parliament.

The Right Honourable the Lord Mayor of London having tranfmitted to the Commander in Chief the unanimous vote of thanks of the Common Council of the city to this army, he takes the earlieft opportunity of communicating the following extract thereof in general orders.

" At a common council holden in the chamber of the Guild-
" hall of the city of London, on Tuefday, May 27, 1794, Le
" Mefurier, Mayor,—Refolved unanimoufly, That the thanks of
" this Court be given to Sir Charles Grey, Knight of the Bath;
" and the officers and foldiers ferving under his command, for the
" fignal fervices they have rendered to their country by their
" able, gallant, and meritorious conduct in the Weft Indies."

Signed,   Rix.

Head Quarters, St. Pierre, Martinique, August 1, 1794.

Parole, MATILDA.   C. S. ....

ONE ferjeant, one corporal, and twelve privates, from each regiment, to parade every morning at fix o'clock, and evening at five, and to be inftructed in the exercife of the artillery; and when perfected, the commanding officer of artillery will report to the general or commanding officer on the fpot, that they may be relieved by an equal number, to be taught in the fame manner, that there may be no want of artillerymen to man and fight the guns on the batteries, in cafe of an attack.

Head Quarters, St. Pierre, Martinique, August 3, 1794.

Parole, SPITHEAD.   C. S. ....

IT is the Commander in Chief's orders, that all negroes belonging to the iflands, who ftill continue with the army, or are known of, fhall be fent to St. Pierre or Fort Royal immediately, in order to their being fent home, and a final fettlement made of their accounts.

Head Quarters, St. Pierre, August 4, 1794.

Parole, Hurricane.   C. S. ....

His Majesty having been pleased to appoint John Jeoffray, Esq. commissary general of stores and provisions, and Valentine Jones, Esq. to be commissary of accounts, for the Leeward and Windward Islands, all accounts in the commissary general's department, for which warrants have not been already granted, as well as those of the assistants stationed in the different islands, as those of the moving army, are to be settled with him, and to be examined and certified by the commissary of accounts, previous to their being brought to the secretary's office, as no warrants for money can be granted on them until that shall have been done. Warrants for the subsistence of the army, and for the pay of the officers employed on the staff, will be granted in the usual manner, on application at the secretary's office.

===============

After Orders.   *August* 4, 1794.

The proceedings of the present general court martial being impeded by the sickness of some of the members, makes it necessary to add more members to the strength of it, that the business may go forward without interruption in future. The Commander in Chief therefore orders a general court martial to affemble at nine o'clock on Friday morning the 8th inftant, at the fame place, and to begin the trial again of Brigadier General Sir Charles Gordon; and which general court martial is to be compofed of a prefident and eighteen members. All evidences to attend; and a lift of them to be given to the deputy judge advocate as foon as poffible. The corps of ifland rangers, commanded by Lieutenant Colonel Toler, to be augmented twenty men a company, making them feventy inftead of fifty.

Members of the General Court Martial.

General Prefcott . . . . Prefident.
Lieutenant Colonel Johnftone . . . feventieth regiment.
Lieutenant Colonel Stewart . . . . fifty-eighth. *Dead.*
Captain Whitworth . . . . royal artillery.
Captain Flood . . . . fifty-eighth.
Captain Taggart . . . . fifty-fifth.
Captain Ingram . . . . fifty-fifth. *Dead.*
Captain Forbes . . . . thirty-fourth.
Captain Pomiere . . . . fifteenth.
Captain Dunbar . . . . feventieth.
Captain Sharpe . . . . fixth.
Captain Harvey . . . . thirty-third. *Dead.*
Captain Gillefpei . . . . thirty-firft.

Captain Blacker .... fixty-fifth regiment.
Captain Lorrain .... ninth.
Captain Hindfon .... fifteenth.
Captain Macdonald .... fifteenth.

St. Pierre, Auguft 5, 1794.

Parole, ANTIGUA.   C. S. ....

THE officers of the army will underftand, that fhould the order of the 3d inftant (refpecting the negroes being returned), not be ftrictly complied with, that for every negro kept back, the officers to whom they belong, and who detained them, will certainly have to pay, not only the full price of fuch negroes, but their hire during the time of fervice.——On account of the indifpofition of Lieutenant Colonel Stewart, fifty-eighth regiment, he is not to be a member of the general court martial ordered for the 8th inftant. Captain Rofe, feventieth regiment, is to be a member thereof, in the room of Lieutenant Colonel Stewart.

h

Head Quarters, St. Pierre, Martinique, Auguſt 9, 1794.

Parole, ANTIGUA.   C. S. ....

THE Britiſh inhabitants of the town of St. Pierre are to be em-
bodied, and to form a corps under the command of Captain Bontein, who is appointed lieutenant colonel commandant thereof,
to be called the Royal Martinico Volunteers. The following gentlemen are to be the officers.

Lieutenant Colonel   —— Bontein.
Captains . . . . James Clifton,
                       Andrew Smith.
Firſt Lieutenants . . . . William Moore.
                       Cayley Johnſtone.
Second Lieutenants   —— Popham.
                       —— Heyland.
Adjutant . . . . Mr. Randal Ripton.

The above corps is to parade at the Pere Blancs, which is to
be their alarm poſt.

All Britiſh born ſubjeēts, reſident in or near the town of St.
Pierre, are required forthwith to give in their names to Lieutenant
Colonel Bontein, of the royal Martinico volunteers, at the cuſtom
houſe; and every perſon of the above deſcription meaning to leave

the ifland, is required to make known his intention to Lieutenant Colonel Bontein: they are likewife required to give in their names upon their arrival. The Commander in Chief has no doubt, from the voluntary and handfome offer of the Englifh in the town of St. Pierre, that all who are able will willingly join the corps of the royal Martinico volunteers, under the orders of Lieutenant Colonel Bontein, to preferve good order, and defend their properties.

F. MAITLAND, deputy adjutant general.

Head Quarters, St. Pierre, Martinique, Auguft 11, 1794.

Parole, CORNWALLIS.

IN confequence of the death of Captain Blacker, fixty-fifth, and the illnefs of Captain Ingram, fifty-eighth, Captain Lee of forty-fourth grenadiers, and Captain Holland of fixtieth regiment, are to replace thofe officers as members of the general court martial ordered to meet this day.

GENERAL ORDERS.　　　*Head Quarters, St. Pierre, Martinico,*
Auguſt 31, 1794.

THE appointment of Captain Hare, of the light dragoons, to be aid de camp to the Commander in Chief, is not to interfere with or prevent his having the entire command of the detachment of Britiſh light dragoons, which he retains as if no ſuch appointment had been made.

———————————

AFTER ORDERS.

THE general court martial, of which Lieutenant General Preſcott is preſident, is hereby diſſolved; and all officers are to repair to their poſts, where they are ſo much wanted.

F. MAITLAND, deputy adjutant general.

Head Quarters, St. Pierre, Martinique, Nov. 7, 1794.

Parole, UNANIMITY.

THE recent act of inhumanity and barbarity committed at Guada-loupe by the enemy (by whom a confiderable number of royalifts were murdered in cold blood, after having fallen into their hands at Berville camp as prifoners of war, and who had become fub-jects of Great Britain, by taking the oath of allegiance to the Bri-tifh government, after the conqueft of that ifland), calls aloud for the following order and declaration of the Commander in Chief: That all perfons refiding in the conquered iflands of Martinico, Guadaloupe, and St. Lucia, and their dependencies, whether French or of any other nation, having taken the oath of allegiance to the government of Great Britain, and who demean and con-duct themfelves accordingly, fhall receive every protection that the other fubjects of Great Britain do in thefe iflands : and fhould fuch cafes of extremity happen as may render a capitulation ne-ceffary, no terms are to be propofed or accepted, which do not give equal fecurity, fafety, and protection, to them as to the other fubjects of Great Britain, as well thofe with arms as thofe without; confequently, no place is to be furrendered befoi_ this is exprefsly and explicitly acknowledged and fubfcribed to by the enemy, that in any extremity we may ftand or fall together: and the Commander in Chief earneftly recommends a continuance and confirmation of this order to his fucceffors in command, as a meafure of juftice, dictated by honour and humanity.

The Commander in Chief hopes that this explicit order and declaration, giving fuch ample fecurity to the royalifts on his part, will eafe their minds; and, confidence being reftored, that it will produce a becoming zeal and exertion to unite for the public intereft heart and hand, in contributing to good order and tranquillity; and that he may expect there will not be any further emigration on the bare report of an enemy's approach, or even on being actually landed; as every apprehenfion of danger muft be difpelled when all are heartily united for the common fafety and defence.

The Commander in Chief, hoping therefore for this effect and conduct from the people in general, does in a more particular manner recommend to perfons of confequence to fet a laudable example of fortitude on every occafion, and to affemble and embody under proper leaders, to act in conjunction with his majefty's regular troops, for the protection of their honour, families, and fortunes, which muft be dearer to them than life.

The King having been pleafed to order that the colours taken at Martinique by the forces under Sir Charles Grey, K. B. and Sir John Jervis, K. B. which were brought to the palace at St. James's, fhould be depofited in the Cathedral of St. Paul, on Saturday, May 17, 1795, detachments of horfe and foot guards were ordered to parade at St. James's at ten o'clock, and marched before his Majefty, who was pleafed to fee them pafs by in the following order:

A Captain and forty life guards,
A ferjeant and twelve grenadiers,
Mufic of the firft regiment of guards,
Twenty-nine ferjeants with the FRENCH COLOURS,
A Field Officer and one hundred life guards.

In this manner they proceeded to the weft gate of St. Paul's, where the colours were received by the Dean and Chapter, attended by the choir, about which time the guns at the Tower and Park were fired.

The colours are fince put up in the faid cathedral church as a lafting memorial of the fuccefs of his Majefty's arms in the reduction of the important ifland of Martinique.

i

EXTRACT FROM THE PARLIAMENTARY REGISTER,
Vol. xxxviiii. p. 329.

HOUSE OF COMMONS.

" *Tuefday, May* 20, 1794.

" The following refolutions were feverally put, and paffed
" nem. con.

" That the thanks of this Houfe be given to Sir Charles Grey,
" Knight of the Moft Honourable Order of the Bath, for his late
" able, gallant, and meritorious conduct in the Weft Indies.

" That the thanks of this Houfe be given to Sir John Jervis,
" Knight of the Moft Honourable Order of the Bath, for his late
" able, gallant, and meritorious conduct in the Weft Indies.

" That the thanks of this Houfe be given to Lieutenant Ge-
" neral Prefcott, his Royal Highnefs Major General Prince Ed-
" ward, and Major General Thomas Dundas, and to the feveral
" Officers of the army under the command of Sir Charles Grey,
" for their late gallant and meritorious exertions in the Weft
" Indies.

" That the thanks of this Houfe be given to Rear Admiral
" Thompfon, and to the feveral Captains and Officers of the fleet
" under the command of Sir John Jervis, for their late gallant
" conduct and meritorious exertions in the Weft Indies.

" That this Houfe doth highly approve and acknowledge the
" fervices of the Non-commiffioned Officers and Soldiers in the

" army ferving under Sir Charles Grey in the Weft Indies; and
" that the fame be fignified to them by the commanders of the
" feveral corps, who are defired to thank them for their late gal-
" lant behaviour.

" That this Houfe doth highly approve and acknowledge the
" fervices of the Sailors and Marines ferving on board the fleet
" under command of Sir John Jervis in the Weft Indies; and
" that the fame be fignified to them by the captains of the
" feveral fhips, who are defired to thank them for their gallant
" behaviour."

Mr. Dundas then moved, " That Mr. Speaker do fignify the
" faid refolutions to Sir Charles Grey and Sir John Jervis."—
Paffed nem. con.

LIST OF THE OFFICERS OF THE ARMY

Who died or were killed during the Campaign in the Weſt Indies, under Lieutenant General Sir CHARLES GREY, *K. B. and Vice Admiral Sir* JOHN JERVIS, *K. B. in the year* 1794.

―――――――――

Killed, or died of their Wounds.

		Where killed or wounded.
Brigadier General Symes . .	Quarter Maſter Gen.	Point à Pitre.
Lieut. Colonel Campbell . .	9th regiment	Martinique.
Lieut. Colonel Gomm	55th regiment	Point à Pitre.
Major Irving	70th regiment	On board the Aſſurance.
Captain Armſtrong	8th regiment	Fleur d'Epée.
. . . . . . Combe	15th regiment	Point à Pitre.
. . . . . . M'Donald	21ſt regiment	Fleur d'Epée.
. . . . . . Grove	35th regiment	Point à Pitre.
. . . . . . M'Ewan	38th regiment	Martinique.
. . . . . . Fenton	43d regiment	Point à Pitre.
. . . . . . Morriſon	58th regiment	Fleur d'Epée.
. . . . . . Forbes	34th regiment	Berville.
Lieut. Thong	6th regiment	Fleur d'Epée.
. . . . . . Booth	8th regiment	Ditto.
. . . . . . Newport	12th regiment	Point à Pitre.
. . . . . . Lyſter	12th regiment	Ditto.
. . . . . . Croker	15th regiment	Ditto.
. . . . . . Knollis	21ſt regiment	Ditto.
. . . . . . Price	21ſt regiment	Fleur d'Epée.
. . . . . . Cockrane	39th regiment	
. . . . . . Manſon	40th regiment	Point à Pitre.
. . . . . . Crofton	43d regiment	Ditto.
. . . . . . Hennis	58th regiment . . . . : .	Ditto.
. . . . . . Conway	60th regiment	Ditto.
. . . . . . Tooſey	65th regiment	Fleur d'Epée.
. . . . . . Auchmuty	17th regiment	Point à Pitre.
. . . . . . Mercer	Marines	Ditto.

Died of the Fever or other Diforders.

Major General Thomas Dundas.

Captain Dally .....
Lieutenant Gale ... } 6th regim.
Surgeon Barton ....

Captain Saumarez ..
Enfign Armftrong .. } 8th regim.
Enfign Caulfield ...

Captain Campbell ..   9th regim.

Captain Twedie ....
Lieut. Perryn ....
...... Wallace ... } 12th regim.
...... Wright ...
...... Miller ....

Captain Combe ....
Lieut. James ..... } 15th regim.
..... Napier ....

..... Cane ...... } 17th regim.
..... Ritchie .....

Major Rowley ....
Lieut. Mewt ...... } 21ft regim.
..... Stornton ....

Lieut. M'Donald ...   22d regim.

Lieut. Garnons .... } 23d regim.
..... Polhill .....

Lieut. Tilth ....   29th regim.

Lieut. Davis ......
..... M'Kenzie ... } 31ft regim.
..... Williams ....

Captain Wallace ...
Lieut. Morndrew... } 32d regim.
Surgeon Taylor ....

Captain Harvey .... } 33d regim.
Lieut. Beaty ....

Captain Roache ....
Lieut. Innes ......
...... Forrefter ... } 34th regim.
...... Wattle ....
...... Nafh ......

Captain Johnfon ...
...... Graves ....
Lieut. Mukins ....
..... Fitzgerald .. } 35th regim.
...... Phaire .....
...... Sands .....
...... Barry .....

Captain Douglas ...
Lieut. Mytton ....
...... Clarke ..... } 38th regim.
...... Brown ....
...... Bawer .....

Lieut. Col. Freemantle
Captain Johnfton ...
...... Shaw ......
...... Purdie .....
Lieut. Burflen ....
...... Atherton ... } 39th regim.
...... Reynell ....
...... Scanlan ....
...... M'Rea .....
Enfign Tidfley ....
...... Hutchinfon .
...... Atkins .....

Adjutant Simpſon ..	
.... M'Kenzie .	39th regim.
Surgeon Campbell ..	
Captain Head	40th regim.
Captain Vignoles ...	
...... Bayard	
...... Affleck	
...... Spencer....	
...... M'Dowal ..	
Capt. Lieut. Jones .	
Lieut. Butler	
...... Graham	43d regim.
...... Denniſon ...	
Enſign Daniel	
...... Kirwan	
Qr. Maſt. Burnett ..	
.... Bruce	
Surgeon Hodſkinſon	
Lieut. Phipps	44th regim.
..... Davis	
Lieutenant Moe	45th regim.
Major Lyon, Deputy Adj. General.	
Captain Taggart	
Lieut. Main	55th regim.
...... M'Kenzie ..	
...... Taylor	
Captain White	
...... Cuthbert ...	
...... Fancourt ...	
Lieut. Perry	56th regim.
...... Hague	
...... Stowell	
...... Warren	

...... O'Hara	
..... Taylor	56th regim.
Chaplain Ruxton ...	
Lieut. Col. Stewart	
Captain Ingram	
...... Hood	
Lieut. Maudſley...	
...... Hamilton ..	
..... Berford	58th regim.
...... Murray	
...... E. Smith ...	
...... Bouchier ...	
...... Tonſon	
Lieut. Cunningham	
...... Sneider	
...... Cook	60th regim.
...... Montmallin .	
...... Belt	
Lieut. Col. Buckridge	
Major Compton	
Lieut. Uſher	
..... Thornhill ...	
..... M'Guire	
..... Wilſon	64th regim.
..... Strafford	
..... Knight	
Adjutant Wilkinſon	
Quart. Maſt. Molloy	
Surgeon Wingate ..	
Lieut. Col. Cloſe ...	
Major Dalrymple...	
Captain M'Gregor ..	65th regim.
...... Blacker	
...... Oliver	

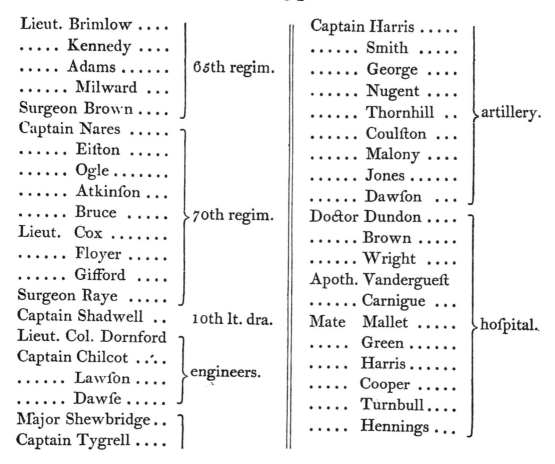

Lieut. Brimlow ....
..... Kennedy ....
..... Adams ......   65th regim.
...... Milward ...
Surgeon Brown ....
Captain Nares .....
...... Eifton .....
...... Ogle ....
...... Atkinfon ...
...... Bruce .....   70th regim.
Lieut. Cox ....
...... Floyer .....
...... Gifford ....
Surgeon Raye .....
Captain Shadwell ..   10th lt. dra.
Lieut. Col. Dornford
Captain Chilcot ....
...... Lawfon ....   engineers.
...... Dawfe .....
Major Shewbridge ..
Captain Tygrell ....

Captain Harris .....
...... Smith .....
...... George ....
...... Nugent ....
...... Thornhill ..   artillery.
...... Coulfton ...
...... Malony ....
...... Jones ......
...... Dawfon ...
Doctor Dundon ....
...... Brown .....
...... Wright ....
Apoth. Vandergueft
...... Carnigue ...
Mate Mallet .....   hofpital.
..... Green ......
..... Harris ......
..... Cooper .....
..... Turnbull....
..... Hennings ...

27 killed or died of their wounds.
170 died of the yellow fever, and other difeafes incidental to
Total 197   the climate.

I was informed by Captain Shank of the royal navy, the agent for tranfports, that during the expedition 46 mafters of tranfports, and 1100 of their
men, died of the yellow fever. The returns of the mafters were given in,
of the men a rough calculation to the above amount was made. On board
the Broderic tranfport the fever raged with fuch violence, that the mate, the
only furvivor, was obliged to fcull his boat on fhore to fetch off negroes to
throw the dead overboard, and himfelf died foon after.

Of the royal navy the lofs was confiderable; but it has not been in my
power to procure a lift of the officers who died or were killed on this expedition.

LIST *of the* OFFICERS *Priſoners to* VICTOR HUGHES, *who were living at Point à Pitre the firſt of January,* 1795.

Brigadier General Colin Graham.
Lieut. Ekins, ſince dead of his wounds } 6th regim.
Capt. Lieut. Smith . 9th regim.
Lieutenant Hurſt... 15th regim.
Captain Stovin..... 17th regim.
Lieutenant Keating 33d regim.
Captain Eiſton .....
Lieutenant Strickland } 35th regim.
Enſign Holmes ....
Enſign Barclay .... 38th regim.
Lieut. Col. Magan ..
Lieut. Horſburg....
..... Dale........
Enſign Divignes ... } 39th regim.
Quar. Maſt. Clements
Surgeon Ormſby ...
Captain Danſey .... } 40th regim.
Lieutenant Holwell
Lt. Col. Drummond
Captain Thomſon ..
...... Cameron ...
...... Thorley.... } 43d regim.
Lieut. Hull ......

Lieut. Cameron ...
...... Tidey .....
...... De Yonge .'.
Enſign Deſhon ....
...... Deliſle .....
Surgeon Salmon ... } 43d regim.
Lieut. Philips..... } 44th regim.
...... Miller .....
Lieut. Hamilton .. } 55th regim.
...... Dixon .....
Captain Owen .....
Lieut. Barclay ....
...... Johnſon....
...... M'Cauſland . } 56th regim.
Mate Bell ....
Enſign Richardſon.. 58th regim.
Lieut. Cudmore.... 64th regim.
Cornet Garſide..... 10th lt. dra.
Captain Suckling ... } artillery.
Lieut. Stackpole....
Lieut. Dornford.... engineers.
Mate Ramage ..... } hoſpital.
.... Anderſon .....

THE END.

For EU product safety concerns, contact us at Calle de José Abascal, 56–1°,
28003 Madrid, Spain or eugpsr@cambridge.org.